I AM NOT YOUR SLAVE

a memoir

I AM NOT YOUR SLAVE

a memoir

TUPA TJIPOMBO
CHRIS LOCKHART

Chicago

Copyright © 2020 by Tupa Tjipombo and Chris Lockhart
All rights reserved
First edition
Published by Lawrence Hill Books
An imprint of Chicago Review Press Incorporated
814 North Franklin Street
Chicago, Illinois 60610
ISBN 978-1-64160-237-2

Library of Congress Cataloging-in-Publication Data
Is available from the Library of Congress.

Interior design: Nord Compo

Printed in the United States of America
5 4 3 2 1

PREFACE

WHEN I FIRST MET TUPA at her brother's house on a rutted back road of Opuwo in northwestern Namibia, I was struck by her story. With her obvious intelligence and insight, she told it in a steady, introspective voice and in fluent English. The story she told me was one of trauma and personal survival that left me speechless; her experience of being abducted and trafficked was the most shocking account of modern-day slavery I had ever heard. I resolved to gather her complete story, including the circumstances and deteriorating conditions that put her at risk for trafficking in the first place, the daily brutalities and routine suffering of being a slave, the people involved, the self-doubt, the ambiguities, and the essential determination to be free.

Yet there was something else about Tupa's story that struck me. Despite having worked in sub-Saharan Africa for over twenty-five years and encountering many different forms and manifestations of human trafficking that were truly horrific, I still found much of her account breathtakingly shocking. Why had I not heard of so many of these things before? And how could this have happened to an individual from Namibia? The country is as remote as they come, a little-known outlier of vast desert spaces and few people with a sleepy, almost aloof quality to it.

There is so much we do not know about human trafficking, despite the proliferation of books, reports, and other publications on the topic over the past twenty years. It is particularly difficult to find personal accounts of trafficking victims. On the one hand, their voices have been silenced by an overall approach to the issue that is based on an amalgamation of statistics, generic categories, and measurable data. The result is a long stream of tedious reports, boilerplate definitions, and legislative watch lists. Any focus on the individual, which happens only rarely, has more to do with how she or he meets the criteria for a specific definition of trafficking, which, of course, transforms the person into another statistic, another object that can be counted and measured, another immutable, faceless category.

All of this brings me back to Tupa and a long, on-again, off-again conversation held over countless cups of rooibos tea at a kitchen table in a quiet town of northwestern Namibia. Her story is presented here in narrative form because it is the way she herself wanted it to be told. Writing her story was an iterative process, and we continually reviewed particular scenes or events many times over as I prompted her to recall specific details, emotions, sights, sounds, and so forth until we both felt that we had saturated that particular experience. As part of this process, I read back to her everything I wrote, and we carefully went over each section together to make sure I had included and described everything to her satisfaction.

It should be noted here that I was able to confirm much of what happened to her by personally visiting specific locations and interviewing individuals in Namibia, Angola, South Sudan, Djibouti, and the United Arab Emirates. I should also note that "Tupa" is a pseudonym (as are all names used in the books). From early on, we agreed that we should not use real names to protect Tupa's identity and prevent her from additional harm.

There were many challenges to writing Tupa's story, but she never wavered in her belief that it should be told. I remember one day, as we sat in her brother's kitchen in Opuwo, poring over the details of one particularly horrific experience of her ordeal, we decided that it was all too much and we needed to take a break for a few days. The room grew silent as I made tea and stared out the window, watching a group of children play soccer. Tupa, sitting at the kitchen table, leafed through a United Nations report on human trafficking that I had happened to bring along that day. When I turned around, she was frantically fumbling with my recorder. "How do you turn this on?" she said irritably. "We must continue." Taken aback, I started to go through all the reasons why we should take a short hiatus. But she abruptly cut me off. "This," she said, holding up the report. "It does not say anything. It is not my story. It is not anybody's story. It will not make people act." She pointed to the empty chair opposite her. "Sit. I need to finish telling my story."

The result presented here is not a statistic or an exposition but an individual account of modern-day slavery—one woman's story of boundless courage in the face of one of the worst human atrocities imaginable.

Chris Lockhart
April 2018
Opuwo, Namibia

1

I watched my pursuers from my concealed position among the rocks. My stomach was so nervous that I was afraid it might somehow give me away. My grandfather once told me that he could always tell when people were nervous because it created visible ripples in the air around them. I swallowed hard and tried to remain calm. The two men I'd escaped from that morning leaned against their battered pickup truck, talking closely as they watched a third man. Though I had never seen him before, it was the third man who worried me the most. He was a slight, almost inconspicuous figure who moved in a soft, deliberate manner, his head bowed as he carefully scanned the ground before him. Occasionally, he squatted to get a closer look at the ocher-colored sand of the dry riverbed. *He is reading the ground*, I thought, and my heart dropped as I realized that the delicate frame and almost feline body language of this curious individual marked him as a Bushman. There was no point in trying to lose them now, I thought; it was just a matter of time. I remembered my father telling me stories of how the South African Defence Force had used Bushmen in this part of southeastern Angola during the war years to search for infiltration routes and water holes used by South West Africa People's Organization rebels. He said they always feared the Bushmen trackers the most because they led the white soldiers straight to their camps. It was why they were known as *flechas*—arrows.

As I shifted my position, I winced from the pain in my hip. I had bruised it that morning when I dropped over the side of the truck and landed awkwardly on a rock. I guess my adrenaline had been pumping so hard that at the time I hardly noticed or cared. But now, as I lay still and watched my pursuers, I became conscious of a terrible throbbing in my right hip, as well as the razor-like torment from the many cuts and scratches on my legs and arms. *This is what happens*, I thought, *when you run for your life across Angola's unforgiving scrubland.*

I had waited all night for the right moment to make my escape. After taking me the day before, the men had forced me to ride in the open bed of the pickup truck, exposing me to the full intensity of the African sun as I choked on stifling clouds of dust and exhaust and fought off swarms of nettling bush flies. I tried wrapping a torn piece of tarp around my head for protection, but it was too small to be of much use. As they snaked back and forth along dirt tracks that seemed barely passable, I was tossed about the truck bed with a collection of empty beer bottles, plastic soft drink containers, bits of cord, and an old, putrefied goat leg.

We had stopped once in the early evening. And though we were in the middle of nowhere, a ragged boy in a donkey cart sat waiting for us under the umbrellalike canopy of a large camel thorn tree. The cart held a drum of fuel, which the two men set upon with a rubber hose to siphon its contents into the truck. They barely acknowledged me as they spoke to each other in a language I could only assume was Portuguese. From his perch on top of the donkey cart, the boy feigned indifference, but his eyes betrayed him as they flicked with nervous curiosity to the somber, disheveled girl in the back of the truck. I remained completely still, partly out of fear but also because I did not want my abductors to suspect my intention to make a break for it the first chance I got.

I had been led to believe we were going to a farm located only a short two-hour drive away. I'd overheard Bernardo—a strange, intimidating man with a burn scar on his face—tell my father that the farm was located near a big town on a main road. But we drove all day on remote dirt tracks that skirted tiny villages and isolated homesteads—nothing that could be described as a town. I never once saw another car. As we drove into the night, I realized that something was terribly wrong. With each passing hour, my worst suspicions about Bernardo were confirmed. Nothing good was going to come from the arrangement he had made with my father.

An opportunity finally presented itself, but not until the horizon began to glow with the promise of another searing day. I repositioned myself to get a better view of the men in the cab as the truck, navigating a particularly dense patch of thorn bush, slowed to a crawl. I noticed the driver's attention was fixed on the twisting path ahead. Meanwhile, the man in the passenger seat was clearly asleep—his head bobbed listlessly from side to side as we lurched forward. Then, when the driver jammed the truck into low gear as we slowed down a second time to make our way around a large termite mound, I quickly slid myself over the wheel well and dropped to the ground. I landed badly and had the wind knocked out of me for a brief moment, but I think my youthful energy kicked in as I dashed into the bush.

I ran as fast as I could, darting and weaving desperately to avoid the needlelike thorns of the acacia bushes, only dimly aware of the stabbing, ripping pain caused by the three-inch barbs. Finally, I stopped to catch my breath; I knew I had to be smarter while maneuvering through this environment—my limbs were already shredded. Standing on a rock, I made a half-hearted attempt to gauge my surroundings, but the bush was thick and the landscape toneless and flat. It was impossible to see or know with any certainty which way to go. I started in one direction before remembering something my father had told me: during the war they used to walk toward the sun whenever it was on the horizon because the light made it more difficult for the South African soldiers to spot them from behind. Walking directly into the sun was also said to be disheartening; people tended to veer away from it. So I decided to alter course and walk directly toward the glowing horizon.

For the next several hours, I jogged, walked, and stumbled across southern Angola's harsh semiarid desert. I pinned my hopes on finding a walking path. During my short time in the country, I had seen few roads, and those that did exist were so broken down and pitted out that they seemed like mere suggestions of what may have once been a possible way forward. Even if I did find a road, I would probably have to avoid it; a road would attract the only moving vehicle in this part of the world—that of the men looking for me. *No, no roads*, I said to myself. A walking trail was the best option.

When I came across a dry riverbed, I decided to follow it, mostly because it offered some respite from the thorn bushes. But after an hour or so, I had a feeling it was leading me nowhere. I knew these dry riverbeds could be misleading; they often petered out in dusty plains of cracked, windswept earth with almost no vegetation. At least the bush offered some shade and, perhaps more importantly, camouflage. So I doubled back and climbed a rock outcropping. Back in my home country of Namibia, such rock formations were known as kopjes—one of those Afrikaans words that stuck with most Namibians no matter what language they spoke or which tribe they were from. I was glad to see that kopjes—though smaller and less numerous in this part of Angola—were still a distinctive part of the landscape. They were the only means of seeing above such a flatland of stunted bushes. This particular kopje happened to be one of those random piles of giant, oval-shaped granite rocks that tourists like to take photos of. My grandfather used to tell me that these were not rocks at all but petrified ostrich eggs from long ago when ostriches were as large as dinosaurs.

Now, squeezed in among the rocks and looking down upon my pursuers, I was glad I had had the forethought not to climb too high or too carelessly. I would have been spotted immediately if I had done so—the three men were only several hundred meters away. I kept my eyes on the Bushman tracker, knowing he was the only one I had to worry about. I clung to the hope that his skills would now work to my advantage and he would lead the men along the dry riverbed for the next hour or so before realizing that I had doubled back. After a few more minutes of observation, I looked over my shoulder in the opposite direction, and there, in the distance, I thought I spotted the slightest wisp of smoke rising above the bush. Were my eyes playing tricks on me? It was difficult to say, but it appeared to be a cooking fire. It was my only hope—in a few short hours, it would be too hot to walk around for long periods of time. And I did not have any water. They would easily catch up with me.

Hope was quickly replaced with horror when I turned back toward my pursuers. The Bushman had both hands raised above his eyes and was looking straight at me. Instinctively, I held my breath and pressed myself against the rocks, counting on the angle of the rising sun to work in my favor. But Bushmen are clever and are said to have magical powers that allow them to see and even sense things others cannot. That is what makes them such excellent trackers. I waited for him to turn away, but it took an agonizingly long time. Finally, I scrambled down from the kopje and set out toward the smoke, where I now spotted several vultures arcing slow circles against the bleached Angolan sky. I could only pray I had not been spotted.

Almost immediately, I came across a walking trail that led straight where I wanted to go. Alternately jogging and walking, I burst into a clearing containing a small mud-and-wattle hut. An old man with one leg sat by a firepit cooking meat in a kettle. I suspected he was one of the *mutilado*—mutiltated ones—individuals who'd lost a limb to one of the many unexploded land mines scattered across the country. There was said to be a whole generation of mutilados in this part of Angola. *He will help me*, I thought, though I could not explain exactly why I thought so. *Instincts*, I thought. *Rely on your instincts.*

The old man looked up with mild surprise as I approached. I spoke to him in Otjiherero, but he shook his head, so I tried English and then Afrikaans but received similar responses. He eyed me curiously now and, maybe seeing from my appearance that I was lost or in some kind of trouble, motioned for me to sit by the fire. He offered me some meat and goat's milk, which I consumed so quickly that he laughed and gave me some more. As I finished that, the old man drew a map in the dirt and conveyed to me that I should continue down the path until I came to another household, which he represented with a stone. He tapped it with his stick and repeated "Inglês" several times. I hoped it meant they spoke English there. I thanked the old man profusely and, reinvigorated by the meat and goat's milk, set out once again.

I must have gone another thirty minutes before hearing the sounds of an approaching vehicle. As far as I could tell, there were no roads in the area, so it must have been picking its way through the bush along the same footpath I was on. It sounded like it was coming directly from the old man's place. My stomach dropped as I heard the distinctive clattering noises of my pursuers' truck. But it seemed to be having a hard time at a point where the path intersected a deep gully; it might take them some time to find a suitable crossing. As I turned and began running again, I almost stepped on a pale black snake with faded white stripes. I recognized it immediately as a relatively harmless garter snake, but it was a snake nonetheless, and snakes are bad omens. For me, it had all started—everything I was experiencing now—when the zebra snake had bitten my brother Timo. That was the moment when everything seemed to change, when the safety and security of my life in the village gave way to the dangers of the wider world. It was when vulnerability and uncertainty came into my life.

———————

"Tupa!" Timo yelled across the compound to me. "Come! We have work to do before the sun comes!" I knew my older brother would want me to help him graze the cows in the dry riverbed that lay to the west of the village. I was good at fetching calves that wandered into the middle of a thick bramble patch, a task that often demanded a young, nimble person who could crawl through the thorn bushes to retrieve them. It had been an especially bad season, and my family could not afford to lose any more livestock to jackals or other predators whose numbers seemed to grow with each passing year. And small calves that got separated from the herd were always easy prey.

I was not quite sure how many livestock my family had lost over the past several years. In fact, I really did not know how big the herd was. Among the people of my tribe—the Himba—it was bad luck to count cows or even family members, and few people ever came up with an exact number for anything. I always remembered the time when the government men came to our village and asked my grandfather how many cows we had. The Old One just shook his head—either because he did not know the answer or in disbelief that they would ask such a foolish question. "Ha, ta, ta, ta . . . ," he exclaimed, a common refrain in my home area—the Kunene of northwestern Namibia—to let someone know that they just asked an impossible question. Yet if the men had asked my grandfather about an individual cow or goat, he would have told them every little detail about that animal, including where it was at that exact moment. Everything revolved around the movement of cattle, and my family—like every family in the area—grazed our animals and planted our maize gardens in accordance with a seasonal round that stretched back generations. Each morning, we milked and turned out our cows to graze. As *okuni*—the time of dryness—came on, the best pastures gradually got farther and farther out until it was time to pack up and move to the mountains. When the rains came again and the grasses returned to the low country, we came down from our dry season camps, planted our gardens, repaired our huts and kraals, and began another year. To each and every Himba, the herd represented everything: movement, wealth, social status, relationships, kinship obligations, blessings from the ancestors—life itself. It was wrong to put a number on such things.

After we had led the cows to the grazing area, I sat beside Timo in the shade of a large, overhanging boulder. It was the hottest part of the afternoon, and the Namibian sun was at its apex, once again beating the land around us into a single, rippling scar of pulverized red rock. To me, there was always an air of invulnerability to the Kunene, as if the only forces that could possibly work upon it were the slow, epochal pressures of geologic time. I always thought of it as a land of horizontals; even the mountains were flattened out into mesa-like ridges called *etendekas*. Dry riverbeds snaked their way in between the mountains and dispersed onto broad, windswept plains that, to most outsiders, must have looked exactly like the surface of Mars. The vegetation was sparse but tough, having adapted to its arid ecology in striking ways. While the various grasses lay dormant and unseen for years at a time, we all knew how they erupted into lush fields of green at the slightest hint of rainfall.

And that was why we had brought the herd to this particular valley—it had rained here the night before. To be more precise, a passing cloud had sprinkled a smattering of lonely drops for maybe ten or fifteen minutes. But in the Kunene, that was enough to encourage new shoots of grass to push through the parched veins of hardened earth.

After the herd feasted earlier in the morning, I could see that the animals were now sluggish; most squeezed themselves into what little shade was offered by the stunted mopani trees and scattered thorn bushes that competed for a foothold in the sandy riverbed. I enjoyed tending livestock with my eldest brother—he was always telling interesting stories or jokes that made me laugh. On that particular day, he was recounting the time he had spent in Swakopmund, the big town on the Atlantic Ocean just south of the Skeleton Coast. Trying in vain to describe the ocean, which I had never seen, he finally told me to imagine a second sky between the first sky and the land. When I asked him if it had clouds too, he laughed and said no but that it had rolling hills that came toward you from somewhere far away, maybe even as far away as America. Baffled, I asked my brother why the Americans were sending waves in our direction. But this just made Timo shake his head. He reminded me that I was still a girl of thirteen years, and such things were too big for me to understand. He yawned and said I would simply have to go see it for myself someday. Eventually, our conversation melted away and we both fell fast asleep.

The next thing I remember is being jolted awake by my brother's cries. I sat up to find him rubbing his foot and cursing. From the corner of my eye, I caught the brisk, glissading retreat of a large zebra snake, its distinctive bands flashing in the sun as it skimmed across the sand. Zebra snakes are common throughout the Kunene and have a reputation for being both aggressive and quick to agitate. Scrambling to my feet, I flung several rocks at the snake to chase it away from the immediate vicinity. I knew that among the many poisonous snakes in our area, zebra snakes were especially dangerous because they could spit their venom at you from several meters away. They always aimed for a person's eyes, and if they hit their target, the venom was potent enough to cause permanent blindness. They often went out of their way to sink their fangs into someone as the person slept—and they were known to return for a second attack.

I knew I had to get my brother back to the village as quickly as possible. But it was not going to be easy; his foot was already beginning to swell, and we would have to walk five or six kilometers through the middle of the desert during the hottest part of the day.

We inched our way along the dry riverbed that wound its way between the mountains north of us and the scorched, windswept plains to the south. Like every Himba, I understood at a very early age that even though this land was my home, it could be unforgiving and demanded care and respect, especially during emergencies like this.

We managed to get within a half mile or so of the village before Timo collapsed to the ground in agony. Terrified, I left him in the shade of a tree and ran as fast as I could the rest of the way home. Within minutes, I burst into our family compound, trying to catch my breath as I dashed from one hut to another looking for help.

Finally, I came upon my grandfather sitting by the Holy Fire. I should have known he would be there. As the oldest member of the patriclan, he was the keeper of the Holy Fire—or *Okuruwo*—a responsibility he took very seriously. He tended to the glowing embers every morning and evening, ensuring that they were always smoldering and at the ready. The Holy Fire was where he spoke with the ancestors and asked them to watch over our household. But today, I thought they seemed to be sleeping.

"What is it, girl?" the Old One snapped. Despite being blind, he always knew who was nearby from the distinctive sounds of their footsteps. He once told me that it was a special kind of wisdom he had learned from the desert elephants, claiming that they spoke to one another through the unique vibrations they made as they walked across the land.

For once, however, I ignored my grandfather, rushing past him toward my mother, Nadi, who I spotted behind the kraal where we kept the goats at night. Even from a distance, I could always make out my mother's long limbs and tall, slender build, physical traits that I myself had inherited. Otherwise, my mother looked like any other Himba woman, with her short leather skirt, tightly plaited locks of hair, and reddish skin that came from covering herself with *otjize*, a traditional mixture of cooked butterfat and crushed ocher.

I ran up to my mother and breathlessly told her what had happened. Together, we located my father, Moses, who immediately raced off with my other two brothers to fetch Timo. By the time they returned, Timo's foot had swollen to the size of a soccer ball and looked like it might burst open. They carried him to his hut and carefully laid him on his sleeping mat. My grandfather barked out orders for somebody to fetch the village healer, unaware that he was already on his way. I could hardly bear to watch.

At that point, Zudongo, my father's first wife and Timo's biological mother, came running into the hut. She cried out and fell to the ground when she saw her firstborn in so much pain. She ran her fingers wildly up and down her son's body, as if trying to locate the poison by touch. My mother grabbed me by the shoulder and led me outside, away from all the commotion. But I knew the real reason she wanted us to stay away: there was already enough tension between her and Zudongo, and she did not want to add to it by being in the way at a time like this.

Having two or more wives was common among my people, but so, too, were the inevitable problems that came along with such a practice. While most family disputes were easily mediated through vast networks of overlapping kin, my mother, Nadi, did not have these relationships available to her, because her natural kin group lived deep inside Angola. I knew she often felt isolated because of this, especially since Zudongo—as Moses's first wife—was traditionally higher than her. Moreover, Zudongo had given birth to three strong boys, a sign of good luck among the Himba. As the eldest of the three, Timo was first in line to inherit Zudongo's eldest brother's property. "When Timo becomes a big man," I often heard her tell my mother, "there will be nothing for Angola."

I sensed these pressures in my mother now as we walked away from Timo's hut. She pulled me aside and demanded to know everything that had happened, clearly worried that her only child might somehow be at fault. For once, I knew that I had done nothing wrong and tried my best to show displeasure at my mother's insinuation, but she was not in the mood.

Over the next several days, the local healer tried to cure Timo by extracting the poison with various poultices and mixtures. There was increasing gossip that it was a case of *embari*, a particularly virulent form of witchcraft used by individuals to kill anyone they thought was in their way. We all knew that embari was on the rise in large part because young men were using it against anyone they believed was preventing them from obtaining money and cars and big houses, things that never used to be a problem because they did not exist before. Yet, even if it were embari, we still did not know who was attacking Timo. I kept asking myself who had the most to gain from his death, but it was difficult to say. Meanwhile, my brother's foot continued to swell until it split completely open and his toes mutated into small black scabs. Everybody could see that the poison was spreading up his leg.

My father tracked down an old pickup and hastily made arrangements to drive Timo to the government hospital in Opuwo. To make the hundred-kilometer journey a little less arduous, we lined the truck bed with a thick pile of old blankets, but given the pain he was in and the condition of the road to Opuwo—which was just a desert track—it seemed to me like a futile gesture.

I knew things were serious when my father climbed into the back of the truck as well. Moses only went to town when he absolutely had to, usually to attend a funeral or because there was an emergency. Like my grandfather, he was a traditionalist and preferred life in the village.

While Timo and the others were away, the Old One appealed to the ancestors for help and guidance. He sat by the Holy Fire for days, barely moving, like a rock or some impossibly gnarled mopani tree. Whenever I saw him like this, I imagined him growing out of the ground itself, with long roots that penetrated the soft sand to some hidden spring deep underground. He always told me that if he did not keep in close contact with the ancestors every day, they might stop listening and go away. "When that happens," he said, "I have to go after them and beg them to return." *Perhaps he is chasing after the ancestors now,* I thought as I watched him over the course of the week. When I threw a pebble at him and it plunked off his bony shoulder, he did not even move or seem to notice. I thought he must have found who he was looking for and was currently in deep negotiations with them over my brother's fate.

Once again, however, the ancestors were either asleep or had turned a deaf ear, because the poison in Timo's leg continued to spread. As a last-ditch effort to save his life, the doctors were forced to amputate his leg below the knee.

The entire incident left our household in turmoil, and as my mother seemed to anticipate, it widened the rift between herself and Zudongo. Within days of returning from Opuwo, Zudongo drew upon the continuing speculation of embari and openly accused my mother of witchcraft against her eldest son. To our horror, the local healer supported

Zudongo's accusations. My mother suspected that it was a calculated move on his part to protect his reputation after he had failed so miserably to cure Timo.

An accusation of witchcraft is a strange and powerful thing among my people. A simple accusation could hang over someone for years, and, as everybody knew, the social stigma that came with it could force an individual into seclusion. I once joined a group of children and badgered a woman from a neighboring village who had been accused of witchcraft. We followed her around for days, spreading stories about her to our friends and family: we said she left the village at night, transformed into a chicken, spoke to snakes, and so on. Before long, it made little difference what the original circumstances were; the damage was done and people were speaking behind the woman's back, accusing her of being a dangerous half person who conspired with witch doctors and engaged in dark and secret matters. Ultimately, she had little choice but to flee the area altogether. And while we all knew that her original accuser was maneuvering to steal her husband and probably using an allegation of witchcraft to take her out of the picture, it did not necessarily make the prospect of witchcraft any less real for us. It was all just part of the local gossip and social politics that defined every Himba community.

For somebody like my mother, who came from Angola and could not turn to immediate kin for support and assistance, Zudongo's accusation was especially dangerous. Nadi's only option was to throw herself at the mercy of the local headmen and elders, who eventually called a meeting to discuss the incident. Curiously, they did not ask either Zudongo or my mother to speak or defend themselves, so both women were forced to watch the meeting from a distance. My grandfather spoke for a long time, while my father sat beside him occasionally adding something or nodding his head. When it was finally over, the men approached my mother and told her of their decision: she would be sent to Opuwo for a year to live with Moses's younger brother, Gerson. I was to go with her. They explained that this would allow things to settle down and tensions to ease. Resigned to her fate, my mother accepted their decision, realizing that it was as good an outcome as she could hope to get. I was not so sure.

When I stood before the Old One, he placed his hand on my head and asked me, "Tupa, would you like to go to a big town with many people? It is a place with motorcars and shops filled with wonderful things. Would you not like to see such a place?" But I could not imagine a more frightening prospect. Taking note of how he called me by my first name, something he did only when I was in some kind of trouble, I tried to look as wounded as possible and responded that I did not want to go, adding that none of this would have happened if the snake had not bitten Timo. I reminded my grandfather of a story he often told me: how a black mamba had come into the village on the day I was born and made everybody flee, forcing my mother to give birth under a tree. He always told me that it was an evil omen. Surely, I argued, that incident was somehow related to what was happening now. What if it was the omen coming true? The Old One rubbed his chin and considered my words, but just when I thought he might change his mind, he waved his hand and said the decision had already been made. Besides, he said, he would make a special offer to the ancestors to watch over me. But given everything that had happened so far, I was not convinced that the ancestors were willing to help.

On the day of my departure, I was angry and hurt. I asked myself how my grandfather and father could allow me to be sent away like this. I was especially bitter with my father. I was convinced that he was sending me away because he favored his three sons. But what could I do? So I left for Opuwo with a seed of doubt planted deep inside me.

2

AT FIRST, I WAS INTIMIDATED and frightened by Opuwo. I had never seen so many shops and houses before. Each one seemed to grow out of the next as they spread out from the town center and clambered up the surrounding hills in a concentrated mass of dust and humanity. I immediately took pity on all the goats that wandered around town, thinking how scrawny and sad they looked. But I was amazed at how many different kinds of people there were—Himba, Herero, Ovambo, Damara, Nama, Caprivian—and how they all seemed to speak different languages or mixed pidgins with strange dialects. It was a bustling mass of people: hip-hop, Hikwa, and Ma/gaisa music blared from the local bars known as shebeens, while children chased makeshift soccer balls through the streets, hairdressers and tailors plied their trades on the sidewalks, customers crowded into open-air butcheries, and vendors sold everything from roasted corn to the traditional drink known as *tombo*.

I was excited to see white people for the first time too, usually tourists who stopped in town for gas and supplies in their distinctive Toyota Hiluxes, the interiors stuffed with all kinds of wonderful and mysterious things. I noticed how they smiled a lot and seemed to be interested in just about everything. Unfortunately, they were always in a rush to leave town, coming and going so fast that I wondered at all the amazing places that must exist beyond the horizon to make them be in such a hurry. For me, a young Himba girl from the bush, Opuwo proved to be an ideal window to the wider world.

We settled in to my uncle Gerson's house, a small cement-brick structure that sat on top of a long, rolling hill above town. The house itself was already filled to capacity with his own family, so we pitched a small canvas tent under the shade of a withered acacia tree in the backyard.

Uncle Gerson was a shorter, squatter version of my father, with a more outgoing personality. He worked as a clerk for the Ministry of Agriculture, Water and Forestry but like many people in Opuwo he also ran a variety of informal moneymaking schemes on the side. He insisted that I attend school, and despite starting late for my age, I adapted quickly. In the classroom, my native language of Otjiherero was spoken alongside English, which helped me adjust to the new environment. And with the support of my cousins, who also attended the same school, I managed to make many friends. I was surprised and delighted to find out that many of my classmates were related to me in some way.

I discovered that I had a real knack for learning languages. I practiced at home by engaging in short conversations with my uncle every morning and evening, mostly in English but also in Afrikaans and the distinctive click languages of the Nama and Damara. He encouraged me to respond to greetings from visitors in both their native language and English. And whenever we came across white people in town, he challenged me to walk up to them and start a conversation, even standing to the side and timing me with his watch to see how long I could go. Eventually, one minute became two, two became three, and so on. I enjoyed my uncle's challenges and found my confidence grew with each passing day. I liked it when strangers responded warmly to me and commented on my intelligence and outgoing personality.

As time passed, everybody seemed to forget that I was supposed to return home to the village after a year. My mother returned on occasion, at first for only a few weeks at a time, but eventually weeks stretched into months until she was spending as much time in the village as she did in town. I lived in Opuwo full time, however, and threw myself into my education, graduating from primary school only a year behind my age group despite starting school so late. By 2005, when I was fourteen and beginning secondary school, I was completely accustomed to town life. The village became a distant childhood memory.

I loved living with my uncle Gerson. A constant procession of visitors came to see him, and his house was always busy and full of life. They often sat in the backyard next to our tent, drinking beer and discussing various business deals. Most of these schemes had to do with buying, selling, or trading cows. In contrast to my father, my uncle was thoroughly modern in his beliefs and mannerisms: He preferred speaking English, almost always wore a suit and tie, and was interested in cattle for their cash value only. He disliked keeping livestock for any length of time and always complained how expensive it was to pay somebody to look after them. He was strictly in it for the money and always wanted to buy low and sell high in as short a time as possible. He dreamed of buying a small truck so he could transport goats and cows himself and expand his operations farther north toward Angola, where demand was skyrocketing. Like everybody, he wanted to cut out the middlemen, most of whom were Angolans coming down to Opuwo. If he could bypass them, I often heard him say, he would double or even triple his profits. Sometimes I wondered how my uncle could possibly be related to my father, who seemed dull and even a little simple by comparison. As I grew closer to Gerson, I began to think of him in ways once reserved for my father.

One of Uncle Gerson's business associates who came around the house more and more often was an Ovambo man named Angel. He lived in the capital city of Windhoek but claimed to have many contacts in Angola. Angel was young—maybe in his midtwenties—and always dressed stylishly, usually in designer jeans and business shirts with an open collar that showed off a large gold chain and crucifix. He even drove his own truck, a brand-new Toyota Hilux double cab with tinted windows and custom burnished rims. It was almost always filled with electronic goods and cases of Tassenberg, a cheap yet popular wine that was the preferred choice of people who wanted to get drunk fast. Whenever Angel came to visit, his first order of business was to hire a private security guard to watch his vehicle. He had an air of superiority about him that I attributed to living in Windhoek or maybe from just being Ovambo, a tribe that Himba were often taught to distrust. He clipped his greetings, sometimes forgetting them altogether, a trait that everyone took as a dead giveaway that someone was from the capital city. I also noticed how Angel fidgeted when my uncle spoke, bouncing his knee up and down or tapping his beer bottle with the large gold ring on his pinky finger. At the same time, however, he was watchful and intensely curious. When I caught him staring at me, which was often, he would smile and call me "Gal Level"—the name of a popular female hip-hop duo in Namibia—and then follow that up with some comment about my physical appearance. "You don't have the big legs and sagging tits of most Himba women," he once told me. "You have all the best qualities of a Himba, but you're long and lean like an Ovambo woman. That is good." By now, I was used to comments about my looks; people around town often referred to me as *omundu omuwa omure*—tall, beautiful one. But there was something about Angel's words and mannerisms that made me uneasy. Part of it was the way he switched from Otjiherero to English when speaking to me, peppering his comments with American slang as if testing my English-speaking abilities. From the very beginning, I thought there was something predatory about him.

In 2006, when the rains failed, people in Opuwo did not think much about it at first. Drought was nothing new. We had all lived with unpredictable rainfall for generations; it was a fact of life. But in the Kunene, it did not take long for a drought to evolve into something serious, a process that began in the bush and slowly infected Opuwo like a virus. To the Himba, each drought had a personality, a life of its own, even a name. My grandfather used to tell me about the particularly devastating drought that had hit the area in the 1980s. Like all the elders, he called it *Kate Uri*—just go and die—a common remark made to those who fell by the wayside as everybody trekked across the desert to emergency relief shelters in Opuwo. Even at its peak, the 2006 drought was not nearly as bad as Kate Uri, but everybody agreed that things were different now. Rainfall patterns were already erratic, and conditions in general were much drier than they had been in previous decades, making even minidroughts potentially devastating. Initially, government officials bickered over whether or not to call it a drought, with most referring to it with vague words like "below-normal to near-normal rainfall." My uncle suspected that they thought the word *drought* would cause widespread panic, but he also believed they did not want to release the millions of dollars in emergency funds that came with such a label.

Meanwhile, news spread about how all the good cattle grazing areas were enduring prolonged dry spells, teased here and there by flash floods caused by violent, localized rain bursts that were almost as devastating as the drought itself. Small earthen dams that many people relied on dried up, leaving behind veiny, cracked shards of baked clay where dung beetles left their distinctive crisscrossing trails. Swarms of voracious red-billed quelea birds roamed the Kunene and devoured everything that was not already dead, and everybody talked about how hundreds of elephants had fled Etosha National Park, pulling up pipes and destroying holding tanks in a desperate search for water. As the months passed with no sign of rain, people worried that there would not be sufficient feed for their livestock. Things were becoming serious.

Our government officials continued to bumble their response. Lacking long-term measures like drought-resistant crops or range management programs—things that people had been requesting for a long time—they relied on people's patience as they conducted a "case study" on the matter. People made jokes about such government case studies. But the jokes stopped when the government told farmers to sell off their animals to "ease the strain on the fragile grasslands." To my people, that was like asking a man to cut off his legs just to get by.

For the first time in two years, my father came to Opuwo. He told Gerson that the drought had hit our area hard and the land was slowly but surely dying. If something was not done soon, he said, the herd would die. He was anxious for any news regarding drought relief or emergency assistance from the government, but there was nothing. In years past, my father would have taken the herd south toward the Hoarusib River, where there was still water and good grazing land. Wildlife also concentrated around the Hoarusib, which made for good hunting. But moving south was no longer an option, not since the area had come under the control of something called the Community-Based Natural Resource Management program and a host of new political entities called communal conservancies. While my father did not fully understand the conservancy movement, he knew—like everybody—how it had come to have a tremendous impact on every village and household in our area over the past ten years. Conservancies themselves did not exist in our immediate area yet, but they controlled all the land to the south and west, places where my father and others took their livestock during the dry season and times of extreme drought. For as long as my father and grandfather could remember, the chiefs and headmen had permitted them to graze their animals in these areas, an agreement our family had hammered out based on long-standing relationships of trust and respect. But as communal conservancies sprang up everywhere, gaining power and influence, my father was forced to deal with conservancy management committees. Members of these committees were brash young men who were not part of the established traditional authority structure but who nevertheless had a hunger for power and influence. My father had never met these men before, and they spoke in terms he did not understand, often producing things like paper maps and "strategic plans." My father could not read, so they had to explain to him how the land was now divided into "management zones" for different activities, such as wildlife, livestock breeding, tourism, and trophy hunting. Grazing areas, they said, were for conservancy members only, so he was no longer permitted to hunt or graze his livestock there. My father pled his case to the chiefs and headmen, but they were now advisors to the conservancy management committees and suggested he take it up at the next annual general meeting. But he soon discovered that these meetings were for conservancy members only. And so it went for my father and almost every cattle grazer in our area.

I watched as my father and uncle huddled together and discussed the growing crisis. My father looked unsure of himself, something that worried me because I had never seen him act that way before, especially when it came to his own household. Uncle Gerson must have seen it too, because he tried to persuade my father to drive a large herd of cattle north into Angola. The cows were going to die soon anyway, he argued, so why not sell them before that happened? With the right connections, he argued, they could make three or maybe four times as much money by selling the animals in Angola. And his friend Angel had those connections. My uncle was so convinced of his plan that he offered to buy fifty head of cattle himself and split the profits with my father.

My father listened to his younger brother quietly as he smoked his pipe. "What would I do with money?" he asked. "I have no pockets to keep it in."

I had heard him say these words many times before. It was one of my grandfather's favorite things to say too. But under the current circumstances, I could not help but think how stubborn my father sounded now, even a little foolish.

Uncle Gerson did not give up, however, and he continued to press his brother on the idea. He emphasized how the drought would kill everything.

"Animals will soon die," my father agreed. "But the drought is only the trigger. The conservancies are the gun."

The following day, my father returned to the village, but he was back in Opuwo in a few weeks. The news was not good: Things were deteriorating quickly as competition grew fierce for the remaining water holes and good grazing areas. My father talked about old alliances cracking under the strain and described how fights had broken out as the wealthier and more powerful families tightened their grip on the best water holes. The chiefs and headmen held emergency meetings, but nothing happened. As the crisis deepened and emotions ran high, groups of armed militia took to patrolling the best grazing areas. The most vulnerable people tried digging *ghoras* in the sandy riverbeds, sometimes spending days excavating pits twenty or thirty feet deep with their bare hands in a desperate search for water. But their efforts were in vain and left the land pockmarked with empty holes. I heard my father say it was as if the desert itself were moaning at the futility of it all.

While in Opuwo, my father attended meetings with other Himba men from around the region who had been experiencing the same problems. They sat under a giant camel thorn tree across from the regional governor's office, discussing the drought and their dwindling options.

One day, I brought my father some goat meat as he sat under the tree with thirty or forty other men. I listened intently as each individual stood and spoke about the crisis. Time and again, their speeches came back to the growing power and influence of communal conservancies. They agreed that while the current drought was severe, it was still a "normal drought," or a situation they had all experienced and come to expect in the Kunene every five years or so. What had changed was the way people were interacting with the land; practices were now written on paper documents and kept in conservancy offices. Everybody agreed that this new way of thinking originated with white men from the World Wildlife Fund and other environmental organizations. The "wildlife men," as everybody called them, had been frequent visitors to Himba territory in recent years, conspicuous in their brand-new safari shirts and hiking boots as they smiled while the Namibian sun turned their faces from pink to red. They were very good at delivering a seemingly endless supply of strategic planning meetings, workshops, and assorted gatherings, and everybody joked that such events would have been poorly attended if not for the free food. But along with the free food came promises of local jobs and income that could be earned from wildlife, promises that were delivered with colorful summary charts and fantastical graphs depicting how much money could be generated by the conservancy movement. By the time the white men left, the land was divided with lines no Himba could see. Wildlife and tourists saw them, however, because they poured into these areas in growing numbers. And while the tourists liked to point their cameras at both the wildlife and the Himba, they did not seem to like the Himba's cows. "Tourists want to see lions and elephants," I listened to one old man say. "Not cow shit." He pointed his walking stick in the direction of one of the "traditional Himba villages" that had popped up around Opuwo, noting how entire Himba families were now making a living from the coins that tourists tossed at them. "These people do not own cows anymore," he said. "A Himba with no cows is not a Himba."

Later that evening, my father returned to Uncle Gerson's house convinced that something had to be done. As they sat in the backyard and discussed the situation, he peppered Gerson with questions about his friend Angel, wanting to know exactly how much money he could make them by helping them to sell their cows in Angola. Finally, reluctantly, my father agreed to the plan. Perhaps, he told my uncle, he would make enough money to drill a borehole near our village to have a more permanent water source. Uncle Gerson assured my father that their Angola plan would indeed make him a rich man, allowing him to not only drill a borehole but also build up the herd again when the time was right. In the end, my father had little choice; his own cows would soon be too weak to make the trip, and the only water holes and good grazing land that remained were in the north anyway. All other areas were divided up by the white man's invisible lines.

But Angola worried my father. His only memories of the country were of his time fighting in Namibia's war of independence, a struggle that for various reasons took place mostly in Angola. It was a dark, confusing period, when Angolans, Namibians, South Africans, and even Cubans clashed with one another for years. Throughout the 1980s, the fighting in Angola was a flash point for the Cold War as the United States and Soviet Union backed different factions with massive amounts of money and weaponry. Cuba and the apartheid government of South Africa became their military proxies—though each fought for their own reasons as well—and both governments committed tens of thousands of military forces to a combat zone that was as secretive as it was chaotic. At its apex, the fighting degenerated into a convoluted mess of political ideologies, rebel factions, and self-proclaimed people's movements. As everybody knew, the war lasted for three grueling decades, claimed millions of lives, and displaced over one-third of Namibia's population.

Yet ever since 2002, when Angola's own civil war finally ended, the country had undergone an amazing transformation, mostly due to oil and diamonds. China had become Angola's biggest trade partner and consumer of oil, an enviable position and one the Chinese were keen to maintain by contributing massive amounts of money and assistance. The vast majority of the money circulated in and around the capital city of Luanda, which became a giant oil-fueled black hole that sucked up anything of substance in the region. And Namibia, a stable country with strong ties to South Africa and historically porous borders, was in a perfect position to feed the beast. Over a few short years, the border regions between Angola and Namibia became a critical link in a vast underground network of trafficked goods. Fueled by equal parts corruption and growth, southern Angola suddenly represented a frontier land of immense opportunity. Smugglers, con men, and opportunists of all kinds poured into the region and established a healthy flow of mostly illegal and stolen goods. Northern Namibia became a conduit for every-thing from alcohol to electronics, clothing, vehicles, and, perhaps most importantly, livestock. For the average Namibian, particularly those who lived in northern towns like Opuwo, it was impossible to ignore the opportunity to make a lot of money in a very short time by trying one's hand in the cross-border trafficking of goods and animals to Angola.

My father was not immune to the lure of the "Angolan Dream," despite the fact that for him the country represented death, famine, and a meager existence living as a refugee in a foul tent city far from home. But now it promised to be a place of hope and redemption. While he harbored a fundamental distrust of the country and shared a general feeling among most Namibians that southern Angola in particular was a lawless frontier filled with criminals and cheats, he also understood that circumstances had changed. Plus, Uncle Gerson had been slowly working on him, assuring him that such risks would be minimized with the right contacts.

But it was the contacts that particularly worried my father, because that issue brought everything back to one person: Angel. He did not like or trust Angel, and the idea of doing business with him did not sit well at all. Like many Himba, my father was uneasy around Ovambo people and regarded them as part of the privileged government elite who tended to look down on Namibia's other tribes with disdain. But everything depended on Angel's contacts in Angola, so there was noth-ing he could do.

Once the final decision had been made, it all came down to logistics. My father needed help driving a large herd of cattle across the Kunene River into Angola. Uncle Gerson could not leave Opuwo due to his job and other responsibilities, so my father enlisted my brothers for assistance. He also wanted my mother to join them since she was from the Angolan side and they might be near her home area, though it was difficult to say, because Angel would not tell them exactly where they were going once they crossed the border.

Finally, and at the very last minute, my father informed me that I would have to go too. I could make myself useful by driving the cattle during the day and helping my mother with the cooking and other chores in the evenings. I begged him to reconsider, arguing that I was from Opuwo now and would be useless in the bush. I would also miss school and everything that was important to me. I asked him to choose any one of my cousins, all of whom still lived in the bush and were much better suited for the job. But my protests only angered him. "Are you ashamed of being Himba?" he demanded to know. "Would you be like the men who are killing us?" I knew better than to even attempt to answer. Besides, I was fifteen—still a girl—and I had to do my father's bidding.

3

In January 2007, my parents, my two brothers, and I crossed the Kunene River into Angola. We were driving more than 150 cows, 30 goats, and 30 sheep ahead of us, a substantial part of our own family savings and that of at least seven other families from our area. The crossing itself was relatively uneventful; the drought had left the Kunene unusually shallow in parts, and though it was January, which typically marks the beginning of the wet season, it still had not rained. As our procession moved slowly north across the desiccated land, choking clouds of dust hovered above us and coated everything with a fine brown film.

While in Namibia, we stayed close to the mountains during the day so that, come evening, we were never too far from a natural spring. Springs were few and far between, usually tucked away in small valleys and narrow gorges, which made them impossible to find unless, like my father, you had at least some knowledge of the area. We planned our daily treks in order to be within a mile or two of a known spring in the afternoons, at which point we drove our exhausted and unwilling herd into the high country to access what amounted to tiny trickles of water that collected in ankle-deep puddles of brown muck. Yet even these unassuming specks of water were like a magnet for all living things; people and animals consolidated around them from miles around. We were often forced to wait in line with local herders or others who, like us, were also passing through with their livestock. Sometimes animals were scattered about for a kilometer or more around a single spring. We always tried to move as quickly and efficiently as possible because the locals did not like outsiders accessing their waterholes. Leopards were also a risk near mountain springs, and there was always the threat that one would kill a stray goat or calf, especially at night. And the drought hung over everything, amplifying both the stress and the risk.

Once we crossed the Kunene River into Angola, we were in unfamiliar territory. Beyond the river, my father had no idea where the natural springs were and did not know where the Angolans drilled their boreholes or if they even had working pumps. According to the rumors, most boreholes in this part of Angola were broken, and locals were not likely to grant access to those that still worked. It was said that they defended their water sources with AK-47s and other weapons left over from the war. On top of everything else, we were now facing the additional threats of minefields and cattle thieves. From what my father and grandfather told me, I knew there were few towns or cities of any significance in southern Angola, just scattered villages where most people struggled to survive. It was difficult to believe that the area was such a critical link for the flow of goods pouring into the capital city of Luanda, where politicians and their friends got rich on oil and diamonds—or so said the amazing stories we heard.

Once we crossed the river, the original plan was to meet Angel at a prearranged location, but he was nowhere to be found. So my father returned to a spot by the river to ensure there was at least enough water for the animals. But as the days wore on, he grew increasingly agitated. He often yelled at my brothers to keep the herd together, and he posted me near the riverbank to keep an eye out for crocodiles and hippos. Finally, on the fourth day, Angel's distinctive Toyota Hilux emerged from the bush, blaring hip-hop music and carrying an entourage of drunken ladies in the back.

A second man sat in the passenger seat, a large, brooding Angolan with burn scars down the left side of his face and around his neck. Angel introduced him as Bernardo and informed my father that he was the buyer. Bernardo was all business and immediately made everybody nervous, including Angel, it seemed, who obviously deferred to him. When Bernardo tossed his empty beer bottle in the bush and indicated with a cursory flick of the wrist that he wanted another, Angel quickly scurried back to the truck like a field mouse to fetch one. Bernardo dismissed my father's complaints of being delayed for several days. "This is Africa," he said in a heavily accented, rumbling English, repeating a common refrain for everything from tardiness to death. My father pressed him to confirm the price he and Angel had agreed upon in Namibia, but Bernardo refused to discuss any details about the transaction until they moved the herd six miles north to his farm, where he said they would find a borehole and plenty of grazing for the livestock. My father was reluctant to move deeper into Angola, but he had little choice. Bernardo whistled and a young boy climbed out of the truck to guide us to his farm.

Throughout that initial meeting, I felt Bernardo's eyes on me. At times, he seemed more interested in me than in the livestock he was about to purchase. He glanced at me repeatedly while speaking with my father, as if trying to hold a conversation while thinking about something else entirely. It made my skin crawl as I found myself staring back at the knotted scars on his face and neck, which gave him a twisted, menacing appearance. I had an overwhelming urge to get out of Angola as soon as possible.

It took most of the following day to drive the herd to Bernardo's farm. The six-mile trek was about the limit of what the cows could endure, and they made a wild dash to the borehole once they sensed that water was nearby. The borehole itself was little more than a rickety windmill connected to a simple pump mechanism that drew water from a pit directly beneath it. A diesel engine, propped up on a cement block inside a small locked cage, was connected to the pump. The only other structure in the vicinity was a small mud hut, which sat under a lone camel thorn tree a short distance away. A string of empty beer bottles marked the path between it and the borehole. Livestock had eaten everything in sight, leaving behind a large circular plain of dimpled sand pockmarked with cow patties. Scanning the immediate area, my father commented favorably on several dust devils whirling about. He said it was a sign that the wind was praying for the rain to come. Fortunately, the wind proved strong enough to turn the windmill and generate power, which was enough to fill the cement trough with plenty of water for our animals.

Angel and Bernardo arrived the following morning. I sat under a tree on the edge of the clearing and watched the men negotiate. As the small group walked among the animals, they inspected different individuals carefully, prodding them with sticks. Occasionally, they ordered my brothers to drag a goat or calf over for a closer examination. After about an hour or so, I could see that something was wrong. Bernardo was doing all the talking, raising his voice and gesticulating wildly as my father stood silently and poked at the dirt with his walking stick. At one point, Bernardo stopped talking and seemed to be waiting for a response, but my father remained silent and simply gazed out across the herd. Finally, Bernardo threw up his arms in frustration and walked back to his truck. Angel continued where Bernardo left off, and I watched as the field mouse spoke quietly to my father, leaning in closely and touching his shoulder now and then, clearly trying to persuade him of something. But after several minutes, he, too, gave up and returned to the truck. My father remained fixed in place as they drove off. I wished he was not so stubborn all the time.

The next three days were quiet but increasingly tense. Bernardo and Angel had vanished without a trace, and there were few signs of life in the immediate area. The heat was relentless, and the wind, which had been sporadic at best when we first arrived, completely died out by noon on the second day, threatening to leave the herd and ourselves stranded in the middle of nowhere without a reliable source of water. The cows in particular showed signs of stress and dehydration. They would last only a few more days. Before leaving, Angel had promised us he would return with some diesel fuel for the engine. But when he never came back, there was no means by which to operate the pump. We could only pray for wind. As my father grew more agitated, he contemplated driving the herd back to the Kunene River, but that was extremely risky and becoming more so with each passing hour. On the afternoon of the third day, he sent my brothers out on a scouting mission to look for alternative sources of water.

By the following morning, my brothers had not yet returned. To make matters worse, we discovered that four cows had somehow gone missing. My father was preparing to go out and search for my brothers when, as if on cue, Bernardo and Angel finally reappeared. Angel looked shocked and sympathetic when we told him about the missing boys, but he claimed not to have seen or heard anything about them. Meanwhile, Bernardo pressed my father to settle on a final price. If they could not come to an agreement, he warned, we would have to get off his farm by the end of the day. He shook his head when he heard about the missing cows, saying only, "There are many cattle thieves in Angola; you are always in danger." I thought it strange how unconcerned he was about cows being taken from his own farm; almost everyone considered cattle theft a serious crime. When it happened in our area, entire villages were immediately turned out to find the culprits. But Bernardo just listened to Moses and smiled calmly, his eyes wandering slowly over the herd before settling on me. Now, staring straight into my eyes, he told my father that he would offer him the same price as he had several days before, but on one condition: he would take his daughter.

Initially, my father did not even consider the offer, which involved me working for a year as a live-in house girl on Bernardo's farm about two hours' drive to the north. After the year was up, he would forgive the debt incurred by the four missing cows and I could return home. Without missing a beat, Angel jumped in to offer additional details when Bernardo walked away to make a call on his cell phone. It was almost as if the two men had worked out the deal between themselves beforehand. But I wondered how that could be unless they had known about the missing cows before they'd arrived. My mother, silent until now, seemed to understand this as well, and she interrupted Angel to speak with her husband. By that point, however, everything seemed to be pressing down upon my father: his missing sons, the stolen cows, the stress of the negotiations, the relentless drought, and the deteriorating state of the herd. He turned on my mother and snapped at her to be quiet so the men could do the talking.

Then Bernardo approached my father and told him that once they came to an agreement, they would go and find his sons. My father stared after the Angolan as he walked away, seeming to put things together in his own head for the first time. Bernardo returned to his phone conversation, speaking in a language I thought might be Portuguese, but I was not sure. His entire demeanor was one of such cool assurance that it bordered on intimidation. Meanwhile, Angel smiled and offered placating words, maintaining that the deal was fair and everybody would be happy. He said they could all go home today and added—almost as a warning itself—that it was "getting more and more dangerous in this part of Angola these days."

I caught my father's eyes when he glanced over at me. I tried to interpret his look in that instant, wondering if it was one of love or sorrow or simply cold appraisal as he tried to work out my worth relative to a handful of cows. I felt like everything I had ever done or been up to that point was now under scrutiny, only I could not be certain how my father was measuring my value. I remember hoping he would recall how I helped around the homestead or found calves that were lost in the bush. Or maybe he would remember all the times he had carried me on his shoulders when I was a little girl, telling me stories about the giraffe and how it got its long neck or why baboons scratched themselves the way they did. I knew those were the best times we had shared together. But ever since the zebra snake had bit Timo, things had changed: I had moved to Opuwo, forgotten all about life in the village, and grown apart from my father as I became more attached to my uncle and his way of life. I felt like my father was weighing all of these things now. As I stood there before him, I wanted to somehow show him that I was still the little girl he used to carry on his shoulders.

But the moment my father's eyes fell to the ground, I knew immediately that he had made up his mind and would agree to the deal. My mother knew it too, clucking her tongue in dismay and instinctively placing her hand on my shoulder. My heart fell as I thought about my life in Opuwo and how in an instant it had all become a distant thing of the past. I could not bring myself to believe that it could all end so suddenly. I turned to my mother and asked what was happening. What about my plans to finish secondary school? I had only two more years, and I was doing so well. What about university? What about everything we had talked about for my future? Could it really all just change in an instant like this? My mother held me and looked beseechingly at my father, but it was clear he had resigned himself to the offer. His voice sounded dull and wooden as he commented that it would only be for a year. I thought he looked ashamed; I wanted him to be ashamed.

Everything moved quickly after that. Within an hour, the transaction was complete; my mother had packed up everything in the donkey cart, and my father was off with Bernardo and Angel to retrieve my brothers. Bernardo claimed they had turned up at a shop about ten kilometers away, but he did not elaborate or provide any additional details. Several boys appeared out of nowhere with diesel fuel for the pump and watered the herd. After that was done, they drove all the animals off into the bush, leaving me alone with my mother. As she prepared a bundle of clothes and some food for me, she gave me instructions on how to handle myself over the coming year. But she was interrupted by the arrival of an old, clattering pickup truck. Two young men climbed out and announced brusquely that they were there to pick up "the girl." My mother pleaded with them to wait until the others returned, but they said they were in a hurry. So she hugged me one last time and quickly offered some final words of advice. Before I knew it, I found myself in the bed of the pickup truck, looking back at my mother as she disappeared in a thick cloud of dust and exhaust. And just like that, I was alone.

4

THE CLOSE ENCOUNTER with the garter snake almost made me want to give up. But God had directed me to the mutilado man, who in turn had told me about the next homestead, where there were possible English speakers. After hearing my pursuers' truck closing in, I knew it was my last hope. I sped along the footpath for another twenty minutes before coming upon a second clearing, this time holding a larger homestead that included several huts and outbuildings. It bustled with activity: two women sat under a tree, chatting as they ground corn, while a group of young boys darted about, pushing their homemade wire cars ahead of them. An assortment of chickens, dogs, and goats wandered about. Dirty, sweaty, and utterly exhausted, I stumbled up to the two women and asked them if they spoke English.

"Oh my child," said one woman, looking me up and down. "You are hurting." She pointed to my arms and legs, noting the numerous cuts and scratches where small trickles of blood continued to flow. The second woman remained silent but eyed me dubiously as she took in my state of panic and disarray.

Relieved to finally find someone who spoke English, I blurted out, "Some men have taken me from my family. I do not know them or what they want from me. I think they are coming now. Please help me." My words resulted in a look of distress from the English-speaking woman, which was quickly mirrored by the second woman after a brief translation.

"Where are you coming from?" the English-speaking woman asked cautiously.

But I did not have time to answer—the sound of my pursuers' truck broke the heavy stillness of the sweltering air. At that moment, the

Bushman tracker ghosted into view from the bush on the opposite side of the clearing. He surveyed the scene before him with eyes that were both attentive and amused, eyes that quickly settled on me with a look of confirmation. He whistled loudly in the direction of the truck and squatted in the sand, patiently waiting and watching as he worked his jaw and spat a long, thin stream of brownish liquid onto the ground.

I turned to the English-speaking woman again. "You must help me!" I cried. But both women were now busy shepherding the children into one of the huts. Desperate, I pushed my way inside and continued to plead for help. This only angered the second woman, who shouted at me in another language as she tried to shove me back out again. Meanwhile, the children screamed and scurried about while a dog managed to trip up the English-speaking woman, who fell backward into a stack of cooking pots with a loud crash.

The general pandemonium was at its apex when the truck drove into the compound. The two men got out and approached the hut. At first, the English-speaking woman seemed to make an attempt to protect me, standing in the doorway with her hands on her hips and speaking somewhat sternly to the two men—now in what sounded like Portuguese. The men hesitated and looked unsure of themselves until the old mutilado man hobbled from around the truck on a pair of crutches. He shouted at the woman for several moments, gesticulating wildly at me and the men with one of his crutches until he almost fell over with the effort. Whatever he said prompted the woman to utter a meek "ooooh" before turning and giving me an apologetic look. She retreated from the doorway as the two men, seeing their opportunity, instantly pushed past her and grabbed me roughly by the arms. As they dragged me outside, I struggled against their hold and screamed, "What did they tell you? They are lying! Help me! Call for the police! Call for your headman!"

But the woman shook her head sadly and said, "These men . . ." Her voice trailed off, leaving only a look of helplessness and pity. "God be with you, my child," she offered under her breath.

This time, the men tied my legs and arms with bits of cord before throwing me in the back of the truck. As they drove off, the assembled crowd stared after me with mouths agape. Everyone, that is, except the

Bushman, who remained squatting in the deep sand, seemingly at peace as he contemplated me with his amused, worldly wise eyes. It was as if he alone understood the full extent of my despair—but judged it unworthy.

Once again, we made our way through the endless scrubland, only coming to a stop when the moon hovered listlessly in the evening sky. The men untied me and allowed me out of the truck. My back and legs were stiff and aching, and my face and arms were burned from the sun. The cuts on my arms and legs were inflamed and ugly. I surveyed my surroundings: We were in a small clearing in the bush that held two meager-looking mud huts. It resembled a temporary camp or kraal that herders used during the dry season. Someone had stacked thorn bushes in between the natural vegetation to create a fenced enclosure similar to something we might build to keep out lions and other predators. Yet there were no obvious indications that the place had ever been used for livestock.

The driver positioned the truck to block the entrance of the compound, while the second man pushed me toward one of the huts. He pointed inside and barked, "Here!" Then he entered the second hut without another word. Ducking inside, I immediately stepped on another girl, who shrieked, covered her head with her arms, and instinctively curled up into a defensive ball. I stepped back and allowed my eyes to adjust to the darkness. I was able to make out five bodies sprawled across the dirt floor. I started to back out when one girl sat up and asked in Afrikaans, "Can you understand me?" Squinting toward the shadowy figure, I responded that I could.

"Come in and sleep beside me," she said. "But do not go outside or they will beat you."

I stepped carefully around several prone bodies and sat down beside the girl. "Where am I?" I whispered. "Who are these men?"

The girl—whose name was Sarah—did not know the two men outside, claiming only to be familiar with a man who had dropped her here the day before. But he was gone now. She said she had been working at various shebeens in South Africa and Botswana over the past six months and was brought here from Maun, a town in northwestern Botswana near the border with Namibia. She added that the man who brought her here owned the shebeens and that he moved girls from place to place all the time. She saw him only when she was being transported from one place to another or when he passed through town and stopped to have a beer. She indicated that he was a powerful man who was widely feared and respected. In Maun, it was rumored that he used witchcraft of a very strange kind to kill or curse people, so most people steered clear of him. Beyond that, he was something of a mystery and nobody even knew where he came from; some said Zimbabwe while others said farther north, maybe even Congo.

I pressed Sarah for more information. Reluctantly, she told me about a time when the man had gotten drunk and showed her his tattoos. They were very strange, she said, unlike anything she had ever seen before, and they covered his entire body. He told Sarah that they meant he was a leader in the "28." Later, she asked others about the 28 and, together with her own experience, gradually pieced together the inner workings of the world she had become a part of.

The 28 operated a vast prostitution ring across southern Africa, made up of different locales referred to as "kraals"—a direct reference to the enclosure used for livestock. Each kraal had a specific purpose. For example, some kraals were specifically used as "capture points," where girls were either directly abducted or coerced into the network by various means of indebtedness or duplicity. Other kraals served as "initiation centers" or simply "way stations" that moved "cows"—girls—from one shebeen to another. Shebeens were the backbone of the network since they more or less doubled as brothels. Some shebeens looked and operated more like neighborhood drinking establishments than brothels, serving a modest clientele of "bulls"—johns—from the surrounding area. These places were referred to as "training kraals" or "primary school kraals," where girls were trained in sex work under the tutelage of a "mama." From here, girls were then moved to shebeens that had a more explicit and hard-core brothel component, which were known as "secondary school kraals." Eventually, girls ended up being moved to the most hard-core locations in cities or along the major highways of southern Africa, especially to anyplace truck drivers and other travelers were frequently delayed: makeshift settlements that sprang up at international border crossings, well-known truck stops, and other checkpoints, including the inspection points located at every gate crossing along the veterinary cordon fence that stretched across Namibia and Botswana.

Sarah explained that most girls who entered into the 28's network of kraals came from southern Africa. But some girls came from other parts of Africa and even overseas, entering into the network from Zimbabwe and moving south toward cities in South Africa, such as Johannesburg and Cape Town. The majority of girls were very young, probably younger than eighteen. Sarah speculated that this was due to fears of HIV and AIDS and the popular belief that the younger the girl, the less likely that she was infected. The 28 also chose younger girls because they were thought to be more impressionable and compliant, making it easier to indoctrinate them into the world of prostitution, a gradual process of moving them farther and farther from their home areas while coercing them into financial indebtedness.

When I asked Sarah for more details about the 28 themselves, she looked around nervously, as if we were venturing into territory too dangerous to even speak about. She said only that the numbers were more like a brotherhood than a criminal gang, which was how many people mistakenly described them. She told me that when the 28 man was drunk and showing her his tattoos, he had bragged that the only way to become a 28 was to kill someone while in prison, where the 28 and other "numbers gangs" like the 26 and 27 were based. He told Sarah that the prisons were their headquarters and that they controlled virtually every one in South Africa, Namibia, and Botswana. They even had powerful branches operating as far north as Zambia and Zimbabwe.

I wanted to ask more questions, but Sarah warned me about doing so, suggesting that it would only invite more trouble. "You should sleep," she said, before lying back down. "I only know that this is not our final destination."

But I lay awake for a long time. It was strange to think that a number—28—could suddenly become so frightening. When sleep finally did come, I had terrible nightmares about the mysterious 28 man.

I awoke early the next morning to the sounds of a truck pulling into the compound. I watched as two men got out and began talking with the others. Suddenly, Sarah grabbed my arm and whispered, "That is the 28 man."

It was Bernardo. Or at least it was the man I knew as Bernardo; Sarah had never known him to go by that name. I stared in shock at the man I had already come to fear. Now, that fear was joined by a growing sense of despair as I realized just how serious my situation was. His distinctive scarring was evident from across the compound, as were his tattoos now that he was wearing a tank top. There was a series of raised bars running up his left arm, almost like small sticks had been inserted just below his skin. They gave it a rough, bumpy appearance that merged with his burn scars. I wondered if they were meant to count or keep track of something, because they were grouped in what appeared to be distinct batches. Meanwhile, his right arm was covered with an illustration of a strange traditional-looking mask, which was itself enmeshed in an intricate tangle of thorn bush branches that ran from his wrist all the way up to his neck. None of these things had been visible before because he had always worn a long-sleeved business shirt. Now they accentuated the grim intensity of the man and added a frightening element to what was already his obvious authority. The other men jumped at his commands, which he delivered in his characteristically offhand manner while speaking or texting on his cell phone.

It was not long before the men herded us out of our hut and told us to get into the back of the newly arrived truck. It was not a pickup like before but a longer truck with an enclosed container, like the ones I sometimes saw delivering mattresses or refrigerators around Opuwo. A place had been cleared for us between boxes of electronic goods, which were stacked floor to ceiling and took up at least two-thirds of the space. To our collective dismay, we saw that we would be sharing the remaining space with about a dozen goats. The animals were hobbled and tied together to keep them from moving about, but they struggled and bucked as we climbed in. As we shoved the bleating animals out of the way to make room for ourselves, the door was lowered. "Sit down!" one man barked as it came crashing down. "We drive today!" I quickly squeezed myself in among the tangled mass of goats and humans as the world went dark.

Over the course of the day, the truck became a suffocating hothouse as it was baked by the Angolan sun and made miserable by the body heat of so many creatures crammed together. The sweat streamed down my body and drenched my clothes. Eventually, the floor became a puddle of sweat, goat piss, and vomit. It was unclear who vomited first, but it instigated a chain reaction until vomiting became just another bodily function like breathing or coughing. I vomited several times, until there was nothing left inside me, and then I just gagged and heaved as I gulped for air. Some girls started crying and praying. Another girl apologized because she had to urinate.

By the time we stopped, it was well into the night. The new location was slightly larger than the one from the night before. There were also many more trees, all of which looked strange and exotic to me; they had large, overhanging canopies with leafy vines that hung to the ground like strands of hair. Gone were the hard, stunted shapes of the mopani trees that were so familiar to me. Nothing looked or even smelled the same here.

On the far side of the enclosure under one of the largest trees stood a small cement-brick house. To the right of that were several mud huts similar to the ones we had slept in the previous night. As we were led to the huts, we passed a huge firepit made from enormous rocks. Just behind the pit was a blackened tree stump with a large hole through the base and two giant limbs that stretched upward, giving it an almost humanlike appearance. It was covered with strange carvings and had bones and little bags of animal hide tied to it that dangled from cords of sinew or string. A brownish liquid dripped from some bags, and a rotten smell came from either the tree or the firepit—it was hard to say which—but it had the distinctive odor of decaying flesh. We filed past this bizarre scene without a word.

I was put in a hut with Sarah and a girl with a heavily bruised face who, up to that point, had not said a word. We were all so exhausted that we simply collapsed onto several ragged mats strewn on the dirt floor. I fell into a deep, dreamless sleep.

It was still dark when I awoke to find my sleeping companions quarreling in fervent, muted whispers. Sarah was trying to grab the other girl's arm, but she kept pulling it away and glancing out the doorway. They were both speaking Afrikaans.

"They will catch you," Sarah was saying. "Did you not see that tree there?" She pointed toward the firepit and the strange blackened tree stump. "They have powerful witchcraft here. They can find you no matter where you go. It is an easy thing for them."

But the girl slipped off her sandals and clutched them in her hands. "I would rather die than remain here," she said. "I will pray to God to guide me." She crouched by the doorway and peered out, poised to make a break for it. Sarah settled back with a sigh.

"Wait," I said, sitting up. The girl turned and gave me a sharp look. "If you come to the police or a headman, or even a pastor . . . tell them what has happened to us." It was all I could think to say. But the girl did not even reply. She turned back to the entrance, hesitated for a few seconds, and was gone in an instant.

The following morning, the truck was gone. In its place were three new men, who chatted as they sat around a cooking fire. Around noon, they came for us and marched us to a small earthen dam so we could wash ourselves. They did not seem to care or even notice that they were one girl short. I mentioned this to Sarah, who replied that she had been thinking the same thing. "A man knows when he is missing a cow from one day to the next," she said. "We are no different. There is something happening that we cannot see. Perhaps they are looking for her now. Her fate is in God's hands."

———————

It was a very hot day, and I slept through most of it, trying to ignore the stabbing pains of hunger in my belly. Like all the girls, I was thankful for the chance to wash myself, but for some reason it made me notice how hungry I was. So I slept to get through the day.

Once the sun dipped below the trees, casting long, stringy shadows across the compound, the three guards began to move about. They dragged several large pieces of tarp over to our huts and secured them to the doorways so we could not see out. They went about their work carefully, double-checking that there were no gaps or holes to peek out of. They even placed rocks on the bottom of the tarps to prevent us from lifting them and peering out from underneath. Beyond a few shards of evening light that sliced through the interior of the hut from gaps in the roof, we were left in almost complete darkness.

After a short while, the sound of vehicles broke the silence, followed by a sudden burst of activity as a large group of people moved about and called to one another across the compound. Sarah commented that most activity seemed to be taking place around the large witching tree. She turned out to be right; soon after, we heard the distinctive crackles and pops of a large fire coming to life.

Footsteps approached our hut, and there was a brief conversation just outside the doorway before the tarp was pulled aside. Two men entered, one holding a kerosene lamp. I squinted against the light, taking a moment to adjust my eyes. The man holding the lamp was neatly dressed in business slacks and a tan dashiki-style shirt. He smiled at us with an open, friendly face. I allowed myself a little comfort in the man's demeanor and neat, almost professional appearance, which made him look like a government worker.

"Hello, my dears. How are you?" he said in English tinged with an accent similar to that of a white man. "How is your English?" We indicated that we were able to speak English, though it was quickly determined that my language skills were much better than Sarah's. The government man—which is how I thought of him now—worked efficiently as he learned which languages we spoke. I was reminded of meetings in Opuwo, where it was common practice to determine translation needs beforehand.

While the second man remained silent during this process, his presence was palpable. He was albino, for one, a common sight where I came from but something that always provoked a great deal of speculation and gossip on everything from sexuality to good luck to witchcraft. Albinos invoked fear in some and indifference in others; it depended on whom you talked to. Whatever the emotion, there was always a sense of the unknown about them.

After determining our language abilities, the government man produced some pens and bits of paper from his pocket. He turned to us and said, "Perhaps you could write down the names and phone numbers of your closest kin or friends. It will help us contact them and send you home." We exchanged glances. I smiled and eagerly reached out for the pen and paper, but Sarah hesitated. Seeing her reluctance, the government man explained that "God had blessed us" and we were being sent home. He told us that we were out of cell phone range at the moment but that he would be leaving for the nearest town in the morning and would call our families to assure them we were all right, perhaps even arrange for them to send money for a bus ride home. However, no one could leave Angola without proper identification, he explained, and none of us had any to speak of. He displayed his own official-looking identification and said he worked for an organization that could assist us with this process. He explained that he would fax ahead the names and numbers of family members to border officials in Namibia and, in the case of Sarah, South Africa. They would then work with family members to secure the proper documentation and proof needed to return home. He said it was a complicated process but everything would be taken care of. A truck would arrive shortly to take us to town and drop us at the bus station. Everything would be ready in three or four days.

That was all it took to convince me. I wrote down the names and cell phone numbers of my uncle, mother, and older brother. I also wrote down my father's name even though he did not have a phone. Sarah, still looking suspicious, wrote down several names and numbers.

As they left the hut, the men pulled the tarp back into place. From the darkness, Sarah speculated, "Maybe the girl who escaped last night reached the police and this is why this is happening." But she did not sound confident. I did not care what the reason was and prayed only that the government man was telling us the truth.

Over the next hour, a strange silence descended on the compound. Eventually, it was broken by a steady, rhythmic drumming, followed by the sound of women singing or humming; it was hard to say exactly which, since they seemed to slur their words together into a single, extended sound. We crouched by the doorway, straining to make out what was happening in the darkness. I could sense that Sarah was just as alert and tense as I was.

Suddenly, the tarp was ripped aside and the albino rushed in so fast that he was behind us before we knew it, pushing us outside with such force that we landed on top of each other in a heap outside the doorway. We quickly scrambled to our feet, watching as the albino rousted the other girls from their huts in the same manner. When we were all assembled, the government man said, "Follow me, my dears," and led us to the firepit.

We lined up before a scene that seemed almost unreal. A large fire raged and shot sparks into the night, illuminating the blackened tree stump behind it. Its two limbs stretched above our heads and merged into the inky darkness. The thick canopy of living trees that encircled us created an elaborate spider web of branches that danced and shifted above us like a cloud of snakes. Around the fire, an eclectic group of people had gathered—some were recognizable by now, while others were new arrivals. Bernardo had returned, looking as remote and menacing as always. He stood on one side of the fire together with his driver, who appeared uneasy as he shifted his feet and flashed a peculiar, nervous smile at random intervals. The three guards were there too, one of whom was beating a steady cadence on a large, empty gasoline drum. Beside them, four women were kneeling on the ground with their arms outstretched toward the fire. They were the source of the singing, which now sounded more like a combination of chanting and heavy praying. They appeared to be under some kind of spell or trance—their eyes fluttered and rolled back into their heads. They were dressed in leather hides and wore numerous arm and leg bangles, which clinked and jangled as they flailed about. I noted vaguely that their dress looked similar to the traditional clothing worn by Himba women, but in this context it seemed foreign and bizarre. The government man positioned himself to the side of us while the albino crossed to the opposite side of the fire and faced us from in front of the blackened tree stump. The man he stood beside was clearly the focal point of the ceremony.

He was a tall man with long, sinewy limbs made up of grizzled muscles and bulging veins. His face was heavily lined and creviced, and he had the high, bony cheekbones and red, deep-set eyes that marked a man of considerable age. His entire appearance suggested someone who had spent a lifetime in the bush. His face, neck, and shoulders were smeared with a white paste that had hardened and cracked, making him look like an older, more weathered version of the albino who stood beside him. His clothing and accessories only underscored his odd appearance: he wore a kind of straw top hat with large feathers that stuck straight out from the rim band, and around his neck hung an array of beads, leather vials tied with string, and a lengthy section of what might have been animal intestines. Beyond his top hat, the only bit of clothing he wore was a leather apron, around which dangled a wide assortment of animal pelts, snakeskins, and more leather vials. Everything swung about as he moved, giving him a sense of perpetual motion that was exaggerated by the rippling heat of the fire. To his side was an upturned box with a cluster of gourds, bowls, and small containers. Several knives and a panga leaned against it.

I knew immediately that he was a powerful witch doctor of some kind, despite the fact that I had never seen anybody—witch doctor or not—quite like him. Everything about him evoked a strong connection to the spirit world and the supernatural. I could not even guess where he was from, certainly not from anywhere near the Kunene or even Namibia. As far as I knew, witch doctors did not look like this. In fact, they did not really have a look at all, and I had never heard of any—at least from my area—who dressed in a manner that might draw attention to themselves. The man before me now fit the description of witch doctors from other parts of Africa where I had heard such magic was practiced more openly and in ways that were believed to be more powerful and dangerous. He was like a character from one of the stories people told one another around the cooking fire; the entire scene was like a nightmare come true. I stared in disbelief, paralyzed with an overwhelming sense of dread.

The witch doctor stared straight ahead, as if he were looking through both the fire and the people before him to something only he could see. He spoke in a deep, monotone voice, in a language completely foreign to me. But the albino translated his words into French, which the government man then translated into both English and Afrikaans. I now understood why they had asked us so many questions about the languages we spoke. He relayed the following message: "You are brought here to be tied to me. Tonight, you will have something placed on top of your head. Nobody can take this thing off. Only I can take it off because only I know what it is. As long as you have this thing on top of your head, you will be tied to me. From tonight, you will serve me like my daughters. If you do not serve me then I will use this thing to kill you. I can do this anytime I please. I do not have to be near you to know what you are doing or to kill you if you do not serve me. I can see what you are doing at all times from any place. This is because of the thing I put on top of your head."

The witch doctor then stepped over to the box and began mixing a variety of powders and liquids. He approached the fire and sprinkled some of the mixture into the flames. As he worked, the drumming and chanting continued at a steady, unbroken pace.

The albino stepped forward holding a chicken and pressed it against the wooden bowl containing the mixture. The witch doctor grabbed its head and forced its beak open, making it swallow some of the concoction. Then the albino walked around the fire and placed the chicken on the ground before us. It took a few uneasy steps, lost its balance, and sat back on its haunches. Its wings hung at a low, irregular angle, and its head wobbled from side to side. It appeared drunk. Finally, its eyes closed and its head flopped over and came to rest on the ground. The albino grabbed the comatose bird by its legs and returned it to the witch doctor, who lopped off its head with a swift stroke of his knife. He grabbed the bowl and allowed the bird's blood to flow into the mixture.

That was when they brought out the girl who had escaped the night before. She was escorted before the fire by two guards, who grasped her arms so forcefully that they were practically carrying her. She made an effort to walk, but her feet mostly dragged behind her. Her eyes had a glazed, distant look, but once she was brought before the fire she gave a start and seemed to become more aware of her surroundings.

A collective gasp rose from all of us. Sarah stepped backward, as if ready to run, but the government man positioned himself behind her, resting his hand on her shoulder and guiding her back into place.

48

The witch doctor examined the girl, briefly cupping her head between his hands and staring into her eyes. He laid his hand on her breast and seemed to gauge her breathing. Apparently satisfied, he turned to the fire and spoke.

"This girl is already tied to me. She is my daughter. But something went wrong with her when I placed the thing on top of her head. It made her rotten inside. She is no good to me now, and she is dangerous to others. Just look at her! She can spread this rottenness to others like a disease. It spreads through the air like smoke. She must be offered to the ancestors to stop the rottenness from spreading. The ancestors have told me that I should make this offering so that you will not go rotten like her. This chicken is not enough; it will not prevent you from going rotten, too, when I place the thing on top of your head. You must be tied to me in a strong way. Just so!"

Producing a knife from his leather apron, he grabbed the girl by the back of the head with one hand and with the other slit her throat in an agonizingly slow manner. As the knife penetrated her neck, the girl's eyes widened and her body stiffened against the guards' grasp. She rose up on her toes while the two men pulled down on her arms, as if struggling to keep her from leaving the ground altogether. Then, as the witch doctor was halfway through his cut and her blood poured down her neck and chest in a curtain, she seemed to accept what was happening, and her body slackened. It was the slightest of movements, but to me it looked like the collapse of something much bigger; it was the moment when she resigned herself to the next life. By the time the witch doctor had sliced her neck completely open, her eyes were already closed and her body had begun to convulse and shudder. Finally, she went completely limp, and the only movement that remained was the flow of blood spreading down her torso.

But the horror was not over. The men laid the girl on the ground and placed her arm across a large, flat rock as the witch doctor exchanged his knife for the panga and, calmly standing over the girl's prostate body, chopped off her hand. He grabbed the severed hand and dangled it over the wooden bowl containing the mixture, letting the blood stream into it for a minute before discarding the hand into the fire. He cupped the bowl, closed his eyes, and moved his lips, speaking or praying in a low mumble that nobody bothered to translate.

Throughout this grisly process, the drumming continued in a steady, unbroken manner as the women chanted and swayed in their trancelike state. The brutal murder and mutilation of the girl had done nothing to break the methodical rhythm; it was as if they had performed the same ceremony many times before.

The witch doctor returned to the box of gourds and other containers and resumed working on his mixture. "With the blood of this girl now added," he intoned, "you will be tied to me as daughters in the most powerful way. I will watch you and know everything you do from this point forward, like a leopard watching in the night. There is nothing you can do to hide from me. It is impossible. Once you are tied to me, you cannot break the tie. If you try to break the tie, or try to run away and hide from me, you will die. It will be like the snap of the leopard's jaws around your neck. It will be a simple matter for me. Now, as this girl was my daughter and her blood was provided for this reason, so, too, will your blood be added."

With these words, the witch doctor and the albino approached us. They stood in front of the first girl, who was crying so hard that her whole body shook, and held the bowl in front of her. The witch doctor fixed her with his penetrating gaze and said, "Your blood will be the blood of my daughter." One guard held her from behind as the albino grabbed her hand and forced her to expose her palm. The girl screamed as he sliced it with a knife. He held her bleeding palm over the bowl and allowed the blood to trickle in. He then cut off a lock of her hair and threw it into the mix.

The drumming and chanting quickened in pace as the men moved down the line. The witch doctor repeated the words "Your blood will be the blood of my daughter" as the albino collected blood and hair from each girl and added it to the mix.

Finally, they held the bowl in front of me. "Your blood will be the blood of my daughter," the witch doctor repeated. His eyes were fierce and red, as if an enraged fire burned somewhere deep inside his head. The white paste smeared across his face, neck, and shoulders gave him an otherworldly appearance, cracking and flaking along the lines etched across his forehead. He had a pungent, earthy smell—a combination of animal hides and herbs—that enveloped me and seemed to add to his power. I felt as if he were inside of me, moving about at will, and that I was powerless to do anything about it.

Grabbing my hand, the albino cut across the palm swiftly and deeply, prompting me to cry out and pull back, which only made the cut worse. He held my hand over the bowl, and I watched as my own blood streamed into the now brownish-pink mixture, coalescing on top with the other girls' blood to create a dark stain that spread slowly outward from the center. I tried not to look directly at the witch doctor, but I could feel his eyes boring into mine as the albino cut a lock of my hair and added it to the mix.

I felt completely hollow as the witch doctor crossed to the other side of the fire. Having parts of me taken like that was the worst possible thing I could imagine. In fact, everybody I knew feared having something from their body taken and used against them. But for a witch doctor like this to do it? I almost envied the dead girl.

After several minutes of stirring and mumbling incantations over his mixture, pausing every so often to make small offerings to the fire, the witch doctor turned his attention to us once again. He held bits of paper in his hand and said, "I have the names of your family members and loved ones that you wrote on these papers with your own hand. These are the names you wrote on this very day. They are here!" He cupped the bits of paper in both hands, held them above his head, and began to half-chant, half-speak in a high singsong voice that sounded entirely different than before. In fact, it sounded just like a woman, which sent an added chill of terror through my body.

He dropped the pieces of paper one by one into the bowl and continued to half-chant, half-speak in his high woman's voice. He then took a small pestle and pushed everything deep into the mixture.

Turning back to us, he said in his normal voice, "Through your blood, your family members will be tied to me too. As I see my daughters, I will be able to see them too. If you disobey me or try to deceive me, I will kill them too. They are under my power now. Just so!" He took a small container from his leather apron, poured the contents into the mixture, and ground everything again with the pestle, but this time in a forceful, almost violent manner. Suddenly, a white froth emerged from the bowl, spilling over the sides and dropping to the ground in foamy clumps. He threw up his arms and yelled, "Now it is time!"

The men approached us again and, standing in front of the first girl, offered the bowl to her. "Drink from it," the government man said. "Do it now." When she hesitated, he added, "It is nothing to do this by force." She took a sip and immediately gagged, but they persisted and made certain she drank a specific amount, which the albino measured using a stick with small notches carved into it.

They proceeded down the line and made each girl drink her allotted amount. By the time they reached me, the white froth had subsided, and it was now just a thick, brownish liquid with what looked like crushed leaves speckled across the surface. Bits of paper stuck up here and there, and I hoped I would not be made to swallow those too. I cupped the bowl in my hands, silently prayed to God to protect and forgive me, and took a sip. I immediately felt like gagging but fought back the urge and focused on getting it over with. The albino measured what remained with his stick, then said something in French to the government man, who then turned to me and said, "Just a little more, my dear." My hands shook as I cupped the bowl again and managed a second sip.

As the witch doctor conferred with the albino, I had a vague sense that they were observing us, as if waiting for something to happen. And something did: first, the girl on the far side abruptly sat down, though she did not really sit as much as drop and land on her crumpled legs, placing both hands on the ground before her and staring wide eyed at the fire. I noticed that something was wrong with Sarah, too, as my friend shifted her weight, almost as if trying to keep her balance. Then I felt a tingling sensation in my own arms and legs. Within seconds, my head felt strange, and I noticed that when I turned it seemed to take a few seconds for my eyes to catch up. A kind of lightness—almost like a bubble—began in my stomach and spread to my limbs. I had a difficult time concentrating on any one thing and wondered if this was what it felt like to drink beer, but I could not be certain because I had never tasted alcohol before.

It was around this time that the orbs of light appeared, fluttering like birds among the bushes and trees surrounding us. They were about the size of soccer balls and seemed to respond to the witch doctor's commands, darting this way and that, stopping at irregular intervals, and swerving about as he called out to them. I watched in astonishment, glancing at the other girls to confirm that they, too, were witnessing the same thing.

"The ancestors have joined us!" the witch doctor shouted over the furious drumming and chanting. Glaring wide eyed at us, he jutted his arms forward with his palms facing out and proceeded to move them around in little circles. He continued this strange performance as he shuffled around the fire and passed in between us. Meanwhile, the albino squatted beside the fire and raked coals with a stick. As he did this, the witch doctor hovered over him for several minutes and did his circle dance with particular earnestness.

Finally, they once again approached the first girl in line. She was still sitting on her legs with her arms planted firmly on the ground before her; she did not even look up or seem to take much interest in the men any longer. The guards came over and laid her flat on her back. They stretched her left arm above her head and exposed the back of her bicep.

The witch doctor said, "From this point forward you will be marked as my daughters."

The albino came forward with the stick he had been using to rake the coals, only now I could see that it was not a stick but a black metal bar with a small disk like a coin affixed to the end. The disk glowed red from the fire. As the guards held the girl down, the albino stepped on her forearm and pressed the disk against the inside of her arm. There was a small sizzling noise as he pushed down and held it in place, which was immediately followed by a piercing scream from the girl. She writhed and struggled against the guards' hold before going limp. As tears streamed down her face, her lips moved quickly but no words came out.

Each girl was laid out on the ground and branded like the first, their screams slashing in turn across the beating of the drum. Finally, I realized that I was the last girl standing. I peered down at the others as they lay in various positions on the ground. Each girl held her left arm at an awkward angle and stared blankly up, as if dimly aware of the pain while simultaneously drawn to something far more interesting in the night sky.

As I was laid on the ground and held down like the others, I tried to focus on the albino, who towered above me. His pink eyes had a cold, detached look as he placed his foot firmly on my forearm. I could feel the heat radiating from the glowing disk. When he pressed down, a piercing pain instantaneously flashed through my body and exploded like a bright white flash inside my head. I heard myself screaming but it seemed far away, as if it were coming from someone else. Finally, the albino pulled the metal bar away and stepped back, and the pain was replaced by an excruciating burning that pulsated from my arm and passed down the entire left side of my body in waves. Like the other girls, I held my arm in an outstretched position and lay flat on my back, staring up at the sky while tears streamed down my face.

My trancelike state merged into unconsciousness. I remember little else from that night. The drumming seemed to go on until morning, reverberating through my entire body and merging with my dreams, which were filled with dim, fragmented images of the witch doctor stirring his mixtures and the albino staring down at me. At one point, the pain from my arm pulled me back into semi-consciousness, and I remember seeing the other girls sprawled on the ground beside me. They did not stir, and I could not be certain if they were asleep or dead. As I drifted back into unconsciousness, I wondered if I, too, was dying, and felt a sense of warmth that was like relief.

5

THE NEXT SEVERAL DAYS were fused together into one long drive in the back of the truck, punctuated by quick stops for gasoline, tire repairs, and short breaks to allow us to eat or go to the bathroom. Like before, most stops occurred at night, usually somewhere deep in the bush, where a succession of boys and donkey carts materialized from nowhere with drums of fuel, propelling us forward into the darkness.

The condition of the roads worsened with each passing mile, while the scraping of branches on the sides of the truck became almost constant. We made our way in a curving, twisting manner that suggested a landscape dominated by thick bush or forest. The driver was forced to keep the truck in low gear as it crawled around obstacles and lurched forward in fits and starts.

Some things improved: The goats were gone, so we had more space to ourselves, though the truck was still crammed with boxes of electronic goods. And the roads were not as dusty as they had been before; they were wet and muddy more than anything else, which was a relief of sorts because it meant we were not choking on swirling clouds of dust. It was also noticeably cooler.

Even with these improvements, we barely talked to one another. Mostly, we just slept. When awake and allowed out of the truck, we hung our heads and walked around in an almost trancelike state. No one asked questions or talked back to our captors anymore. Each girl seemed resigned to her fate, at least for the time being.

It had been like this ever since the morning after the witchcraft ceremony. The government man—the only individual from the witchcraft party who remained behind—gathered us together and made certain we understood the consequences of what had happened to us, including the risks to ourselves and members of our family if we ever tried to run away or defy our "new father." He reminded us of the mysterious thing on top of our heads, patting his own head and smiling knowingly, as if he could actually see whatever it was floating ominously above us. "He is always watching," he said.

But in the end he did not have to worry. I knew that all the girls felt as I did: that we were now living under a curse so powerful that there was simply nothing we could do. I not only believed it but felt it too; it was like a heavy, living mass deep inside me that threatened to grow roots and suck me into the ground. I felt like my body, my actions, my entire being were no longer my own. I was convinced that the effects of whatever they did to me that night were permanent; they would be with me for as long as I lived.

As I was pitched about in the blackness of the truck, I thought about my grandfather and how, whenever he spoke about witchcraft, he used to say that Africa was the land of no accidents. It was often all he said on the matter; it was enough for him. And I accepted it unquestioningly. For me, witchcraft was real, it was proximate, it was part of my everyday life. I grew up surrounded by witchcraft in one form or another. Zudongo's accusation of witchcraft against my mother was a large part of why I was here now. When people from my village became ill or suffered some misfortune, the first thing they did was go to the local healer, who never failed to diagnose the cause of their suffering by identifying who was witching them. The whole idea that witchcraft existed was due in large part to the number of healers who so easily identified witchcraft as the cause of one's misfortune. Healers and witches were two sides of the same coin. The only difference was that while healers were public figures who were widely respected, witches were hard to identify; nobody actually claimed to be one. Even those who were accused of witchcraft were just that—accused. If healers represented the good and public side of the spirit world, then witches were their evil and secretive counterparts. So now, to have seen one like this, out in the open, was beyond anything I could have imagined. It was beyond words. It was beyond life itself.

I knew Sarah was feeling the same way. As we sat together under a tree during a short break, she confided in me, suggesting that there were only two paths before us now. "One is this . . ." she said, motioning toward the truck but unable to find the words to describe it. "And the other is to kill ourselves. But how we can do that? It is a sin." As she spoke, she fingered the burn on the back of her arm. We all carried the same crude mark now: a long, wavy line like a snake with three dots below and one above. No one knew what it meant.

At one point, we stopped at a camp next to a slow-moving, brownish river. We were permitted to bathe, but we worried about crocodiles and hippos and, given the strange surroundings, creatures we might not even know about. As we remained on the bank cautiously splashing ourselves, a second truck arrived, and the men transferred goods into it under the watchful eyes of Bernardo. After that task was complete, he approached our little group and reminded us once again of the consequences that would befall us if we attempted to run away. It became clear that he was passing us on to the crew of the new truck. He made a point of taking me aside and speaking directly to me. "You are not just any girl," he told me, his twisted face as cold and inflexible as ever. "You are to go to a special place. Do not run again, or I will find you and cut your head off myself."

A cold chill ran down my spine as Bernardo turned and signaled his driver that it was time to go. I did not doubt for a second that he was capable of doing exactly what he said. I realized now why I had not met the same fate as the other girl who had run away. Unlike that girl—and possibly everybody else—I had been singled out for this so-called special place. As I agonized over my fate, the new crew, which included one African man and three Chinese, herded us toward the waiting truck.

In some ways, the fact that the Chinese were involved in whatever was happening now was not surprising to me. Chinese people could be found all across Africa these days, especially when it came to business. They had set up "China Shops" just about anywhere you went; there were many in Opuwo and throughout the Kunene. Sometimes the "shop" was little more than the actual shipping container sent directly from China, packed to the hilt with plastic toys, fake jewelry, cheap sunglasses, and knock-off soccer jerseys.

My uncle Gerson hated the Chinese; he ranted about their poor treatment of Africans and how they did nothing for local communities. Like many people, he believed they were only allowed to enter Namibia and other countries because, over the past decade, the Chinese government had poured so much money into big projects like roads, bridges, soccer stadiums, and government buildings. These were bribes, my uncle argued, so China could steal our most precious resources: oil, trees, animals, and minerals. *And girls*, I thought. Perhaps the truck I was traveling in now was just another China Shop.

Of the three Chinese men who accompanied us on the next leg of our journey, only one spoke English, though he did so in a manner that sounded strange to me. I thought I recognized some French words too, but I could not be certain. Whatever language it was, the African man, who called himself Alieu, understood it well enough, though he seemed to find it funny, smirking and tittering at almost everything his Chinese colleagues said.

We resumed a mind-numbing pattern of long, jarring drives punctuated by brief, uneventful stops. By now, we were familiar with the different types of stops and way stations. Fuel stops, for example, always occurred during the day; we learned to anticipate them as the truck turned off the main road and drove for thirty minutes or so on a secondary track, its poor condition making it easy to identify. The ever-present donkey cart waited for us with a barrel full of fuel. It was almost always driven by a small boy who tried not to gawk at us too openly. Petrol boys—as I came to think of them—seemed to know that part of their job was to remain completely silent; few ever spoke unless spoken to first. It seemed like they knew that what they were seeing was not to be discussed. As for overnight stops, most took place in secluded, well-hidden locations that were clearly designed to accommodate small groups of people on a temporary basis. There were usually a few tattered sleeping huts for us girls and a main house or hut for the men. Sometimes we slept on a simple raised platform with a slanted roof made of grass or whatever happened to be on hand. In most cases, a fence of thorn bushes or branches lined the perimeter. After the truck was positioned to block the entrance, two or three individuals took turns as guards throughout the night. One of our overnight stops appeared to be another witchcraft site; it looked eerily similar to the place where we had undergone our own ordeal. It included an oversized firepit, a table made of large rocks, and even bits of animal hide and bones dangling from a nearby tree. Petrified at the thought of being subjected to another ritual, I barely slept that night. I came to the conclusion that some places were specifically designed to serve as special witchcraft sites, where girls were subjected to a ritual similar to our own. I wondered if it was something that every new girl experienced at the beginning, which made me realize that I was now part of a larger and more organized world than I had previously thought.

During this particular stretch, the truck's contents underwent constant turnover as cargo was loaded and unloaded at different overnight stops or transferred directly from one truck to another during the day. This included the human cargo as well; girls were dropped off, picked up, and transferred between trucks and locations on a regular basis. I noticed how all the girls were practically interchangeable: they were all very young, in most cases younger than myself, and they were all pretty. They were so similar in appearance that it was impossible to understand why some were left behind, some were transferred to another truck, or some, like myself, remained with the same truck as it drove on from one location to the next. Sometimes, I was joined with as few as three girls. During other stretches, however, the truck was packed with more than a dozen bodies.

As the days wore on, the landscape changed dramatically. At one point, we climbed in elevation for many kilometers, the truck grinding away slowly but steadily, until we reached a vast plateau, where the daily fuel stops offered a good vantage point of the surrounding countryside. I marveled at the lush, rolling hills and deep valleys. I had never seen such dense growth before or so many different shades of green. It was like a vast patchwork quilt had been laid across the land. Farms dotted the surrounding hills, and thick clumps of trees grew in tight clusters, sometimes fanning out in thin tendrils that wove their way in between the farms. I watched as people walked along a network of footpaths between farms, going about their daily business in a manner that made me ache for home.

For the most part, the Chinese men ignored us, rarely communicating beyond gestures or simple commands. They seemed intent on getting to the day's destination as quickly as possible. Alieu, on the other hand, tried to start conversations with me on several occasions, but the Chinese men usually put a stop to it by sending him away to collect firewood, fix a tire puncture, or attend to some other job. Meanwhile, the girls were expected to do all the cooking and cleaning. But our duties were frequently disrupted by illness, which everybody blamed on the cooler temperatures and damp air. Myself, I fell into a subdued daily routine as we made our way over and around the endless hills and passed through long stretches of dense forest that became more and more ominous.

After a particularly long day of driving that lasted well into the night, the truck lurched to a stop and Alieu threw open the door. An impenetrable forest loomed over us on all sides. I had never seen such tall trees before; the tops were invisible as they faded into the humid night. The murky gloom of the forest seemed to bleed into the air. I shuddered as I took in my new surroundings.

We were on the edge of a circular clearing hacked out of the forest. A few stark, sickly looking trees remained in the middle, stripped of their branches and adorned with three floodlights, which cast a pasty, yellowish glare in every direction. A mass of insects and bats hummed and buzzed around the lights in a frenzied cloud. Peering at us disinterestedly, a man with a rifle sat on a rough platform in the center of the clearing, dangling his legs and smoking a cigarette. The rest of the compound was dotted with bleak tree stumps and clusters of tangled bushes, where stray bits of garbage collected. A long and crudely built brick building with six or seven narrow slits for doorways dominated the opposite side of the clearing. Two more men stood chatting in front of the building, each holding a rifle.

The three Chinese men set off to their right toward a cluster of smaller buildings and canvas tents. Left alone with the human cargo, Alieu wearily motioned us forward toward the dormitory building. But walking even that short distance proved to be a challenge in the slippery mix of mud and clay that made up the forest floor. I was forced to take my shoes off as I picked my way across the compound.

Alieu conferred with the two guards before parceling us out into different rooms. I was separated from the rest of the group and directed to a room at the end of the building. I had to duck my head and turn sideways to pass through the doorway, where I was confronted with a roomful of more girls strewn about the floor. I made my way to the opposite side of the room and lay down, falling asleep almost immediately.

The next morning began early as a large group of girls was herded into two waiting trucks. From my vantage point at the doorway, I counted at least twenty individuals. Each one looked younger than myself. I estimated that at least forty girls remained behind. Of these, about a dozen were so sick that they were quarantined from the others and placed together in a room at the far end of the dormitory.

Before long, Alieu and one of the Chinese men were making visits to each room, carefully choosing three or four girls at a time and leading them away to a small building garnished with an assortment of satellite dishes and radio antennae. They passed me over with little more than a glance until the very end, when I was finally ushered out and made to join a second girl. I noticed that she was about my age and of similar height and build. We could have been sisters.

The building we were brought to was sparsely furnished, with a desk, several computers, and a video camera set on a tripod. Another Chinese man, short and heavily muscled, sat behind the desk. He immediately stood up when he saw me, cutting off his companion midsentence and brushing past him to take a closer look at me. I had a distinct feeling he was the big boss, the one who made everybody else I'd met so far seem like nothing. While he was a good six inches shorter than me, he carried himself with such authority that my height only made me feel more exposed. He grasped my forearm and said in perfect English, "My name is Ming. Please turn around for me." He studied me silently from behind for a minute or so before saying, "Face me, please." I turned again, and he commanded, "Open your mouth and show me your teeth." He took a step closer and peered inside my mouth, nodding approvingly. He stepped back and appraised me once again. It felt like a medical exam.

"How is your English?" Ming asked.

"It is very good," I responded.

"Point to my computer with your right hand while placing your left hand on top of your head," he said very quickly.

I hesitated. "Excuse me?"

Ming simply stared at me.

Feeling more than a little foolish, I did as commanded. When the other girl looked at me strangely, I realized that she had not understood the man.

Ming smiled vaguely and said, "OK, fine. I wanted to make sure that you understood my English."

"I understood you very well. I told you that I could speak English. Did you not believe me? I speak it better than all these men who brought me here, including your other Chinamen." It felt good to speak up to this man who had made me open my mouth and inspected me like I was nothing. And now that I knew he was a man of some authority, I felt somewhat emboldened. Besides, I asked myself, what was there to lose?

But Ming only nodded and seemed to approve of me even more. I felt the urge to continue and demanded to know where they were taking me.

The other Chinese man said something in an entirely new language I had never heard before, but Ming shook his head in response, waving his hand dismissively. He continued to look at me approvingly.

Ignoring my own questions, he asked me how old I was. I told him I was sixteen.

"Are you a virgin?" he then asked.

Momentarily taken aback, I responded that I was, adding that I was not some prostitute off the streets. I told Ming I was in secondary school in Opuwo and had plans to attend university. But he simply repeated his question and asked me again if I was certain that I was a virgin, warning me that I should not lie because they would be testing me for HIV.

"I have just told you that I am a virgin," I said angrily. "How can I be a virgin and have AIDS?"

Ming flashed his vague smile before turning to his colleague and speaking again in their strange language. He turned back to me and asked what tribe I was from.

"I am Himba. Himba from Namibia."

"You are a full Himba? No mix?"

"Yes. I am full Himba."

He nodded and clapped his hands together. "OK, good. Let's proceed."

The second man left the room and returned several minutes later accompanied by an African woman. She made me sit down and, moving quickly, tied a small bit of rope across my bicep, tapped the crook of my arm, and drew two small vials of blood.

Producing a cloth measuring tape, the second Chinese man took various measurements of my body, relaying the information to Ming, who entered it into his computer.

They made me stand in front of the video camera as Ming gave me a piece of paper. "Read this," he said. Stepping behind the video camera, he filmed me as I read several paragraphs. They were a series of unrelated sentences in English that made no real sense. I had no trouble reading them. He told me to read them again, but louder.

He continued filming as he asked me a series of questions: *What is your name? Where are you from? What tribe are you? How old are you? Are you a virgin? Do you have siblings? Describe your life. Did you live in a village? Where did you learn your English?* Some questions were repetitive. It seemed like they only wanted to hear me speak. If I hesitated or my responses were deemed too short, Ming gestured for me to continue speaking. I had no idea what he was looking for, so I said anything that came to mind. I talked about my family and how much I missed them. I spoke about my plans to go to university. I said over and over again how I just wanted to go home. But Ming did not seem to care as he stared at his video camera. To him, the words were just rocks falling from my mouth, things without meaning or significance.

After the video interview, the woman led me to a small building with a makeshift shower and motioned for me to strip and wash myself. I had not washed for many days, so I did not hesitate and handed the woman my clothes. Before leaving, she pointed to a few strips of hide skins laid out on a drum beside the shower. I was unsure what to make of them.

When the woman returned, she looked irritated and snatched up the skins. She began fitting them around my waist, and it eventually became clear to me that I was expected to wear them somehow. But they were ridiculously small and made me feel more exposed than if I were wearing nothing at all. It took some adjusting just to keep my private parts covered. There was nothing for my breasts, however, and after some consideration the woman even removed several pieces of hide from the back to leave my buttocks exposed.

She then spread some kind of grease or animal fat over my entire body. It gave off a musty, almost metallic odor similar to blood. Afraid that I was being prepared for another ritual, my mind raced through all the possibilities. I thought about making a run for it, but where would I go? I would never survive in the forest; they would catch me and beat me, perhaps even kill me. Something about the place made me feel I had little choice but to accept my circumstances. If they were, in fact, preparing me for some kind of sacrifice, I thought, I could only hope they would kill me quickly.

As all of these thoughts raced through my mind, the woman produced lipstick and other cosmetics, motioning for me to hold still as she applied everything in a clumsy manner. It was a strange way to prepare somebody for a sacrifice, I thought.

We returned to the video room, where Ming was speaking in English on the phone. When he saw me, he said to the person on the other end of the line, "She is here now. I think you will be pleased with her." He described how beautiful I was and how well I spoke English. He said I was a "true Himba from the village" and "a rare one—very special."

The woman positioned me in front of the video camera once again. Ming began filming, asking the person on the phone if he was receiving it. Ming told me to turn around slowly. When I was halfway around, he told me to stop. "She is very nice from behind, yes?" he asked. He described how tall I was. And young. He mentioned that I would stay slim for many years. He repeated how nice I was from behind.

I realized that I was being put on display for the caller on the other end of the line. That person, whoever it was, was my . . . buyer. Ming repeated phrases like "as you ordered" or "just like you wanted" and made it clear that my mysterious new owner wanted a young, tall, slim girl—possibly even a Himba girl specifically. Now that I had been ordered and was in the process of being delivered to my new owner, he wanted to inspect the product first. I was oiled, dressed in hide skins, and smeared with makeup to make me look both traditional and desirable. Maybe my buyer wanted some kind of primitive whore, I thought.

Looking pleased with himself, Ming finished his phone conversation and dismissed me with a wave, but not before giving me a sharp, cold stare. I could sense his desire for me, having seen that look in the eyes of many men before, back in Opuwo. But there was something more remote and alien in Ming's eyes, like a mix of desire and indifference.

The woman led me to a different building this time—a tiny, one-room structure—making sure to lock the door behind her as she left. I sat on the edge of a small bed, which was the only piece of furniture in the room, and felt almost guilty as I ran my hands across the crisp, clean sheets. It had been a long time since I had slept on a real mattress, so I lay down and fell asleep almost instantly.

I awoke to the sounds of the door being unlocked, realizing with a start that I must have slept all day. The room was dark now, except for the yellow glare from the floodlights that slanted in from a large vent above the bed. Somewhere in the compound, I heard the high, tinny sounds of hip-hop music being played over a portable radio.

Ming entered the room and closed the door behind him. His face was blank. Stepping over to the bed, he stood over me and motioned for me to get up. As soon as I was on my feet, he slapped me across the face with such force that I staggered and lost my balance, falling against the back wall. My head throbbed and tears immediately streamed down my cheeks. I drew my knees up and covered my head with my arms.

A second blow did not come, but I sensed Ming standing over me, looking down at me in silence. As the ringing in my head slowly subsided, I glanced up at him.

"Stand up, girl," he said in a hollow, lifeless voice. When I stood up he immediately set upon me, clutching and grabbing at my body in a frenzied burst of energy that truly shocked me. He threw me onto the bed and ripped off the tiny hide skins that until then had seemed so inadequate. Now, without them, I felt completely powerless. Knowing what was about to happen, I froze with fear and humiliation. I could not move. My whole body went numb.

There was nothing sexual about what happened that night, nothing that even remotely made it like sex. It was pain and violence. It was garbage and spit and shit. My strongest memory of the night itself was the foul odor of the man himself, who had clearly not washed for some time and smelled like the sour, rotting jungle around us. His stench was that of an animal: raw and offensive.

When I think back on that night now, it is impossible for me to separate it from another childhood memory. I cannot remember if I was thinking of this memory on the night itself, but to me it makes no difference; the two have become so intertwined that it is as if they have become one and the same, like the way a snake coils around its prey.

I must have been around ten. I was collecting firewood by myself in a dry riverbed near my village, when the afternoon's silence was suddenly broken by the piercing screams and guttural barks of a large troop of baboons. Curious, I followed a bend in the riverbed toward the commotion. I stepped carefully because I thought the baboons might have spotted a leopard, but instead I came upon some kind of internal quarrel among the baboons themselves. The focal point of all the excitement was a female who had been chased high up a large, overhanging tree by an extremely aggressive and ferocious-looking male.

I have always been afraid of baboons. They are savage, violent things, constantly shrieking and fighting or hanging around villages, destroying gardens or waiting for the right moment to steal your food. To this day, I am uneasy with their humanlike appearance and mannerisms, an association that my grandfather reinforced with stories of how they were once children who had become lost in the bush. In the Kunene, the males are twice the size of females; they are larger than most dogs and easily come up to a man's waist. They constantly fight one another to assert their authority, ripping at each other's faces with their long, razor-sharp teeth until a clear winner emerges, who is then free to pursue the females as he pleases.

In this instance, the dominant male had chased and harassed one of the females until she was forced to climb the tree. Now, the two were in the highest branches, balancing precariously above the rocks lining the riverbed below. I climbed the bank to get a better look and watched as the male bit and violently shook the female, ripped the hair from her head and body, and pushed her closer and closer to the outer edges of the branches. It must have been going on for some time, because she was a mess; most of the hair on her head had been ripped out, one eye was swollen shut, and there was a gash across her nose all the way to the bone. Her tail was bit almost in two. She was covered in blood and screaming for her life. Meanwhile, the rest of the troop, which must have consisted of at least twenty or thirty other baboons, ran around the base of the tree, wailing and screaming and howling in a manner I had never seen before. Some were throwing sand in the air and beating their fists on the rocks in distress. It was like they had all lost their minds. It was a scene of total madness and chaos.

Finally, the male pushed the female to the very edge of the branch until it could no longer bear her weight. She slipped off and twisted in midair, just barely grabbing the branch with one hand. She extended her other hand to the male in one final, desperate appeal for mercy, but he lunged forward with a hiss and bit it with his giant canines. She fell from the tree and landed with a horrifying thud on the rocks below.

I thought there was no way she could have survived such a fall. But to my surprise, she began to move after a minute or so and eventually stood up on very shaky legs. The fall had resulted in even more horrifying injuries: her entrails were now spilling out of her anus.

When the males of the group all surged forward to grab her, it dawned on me that she was in heat. Despite everything, they were still trying to mate with her. I could hardly believe that the urge was so strong in them that they would pursue such a broken, wretched creature. As the female desperately tried to fend off her new attackers on the ground, the dominant male was making his way down from the tree.

Upon reaching the scene on the ground, he quickly chased away the other males. They retreated a short distance away, still howling and carrying on, whether out of excitement or agitation, I did not know. The females were clearly agitated and continued to scream and scream. The sound was overwhelming. But the injured female was now silent. She simply stood there, dazed, bloody, her insides pouring from her to form a heaping, steaming mess on the sandy riverbed. I saw that half her tail had snapped off, and she held one arm at an awkward angle, as if it had broken in several places. Knowing that she was completely his now, the big male approached her from behind, casually pushed aside her entrails, and mounted her.

That is the memory I have in my head when I think about the night I lost my virginity and my childhood was stolen from me. As for the night itself, I cannot remember everything, only bits and pieces. Toward the end, when Ming had finished with me, I remember fixing my gaze on the yellow light in the far corner of the room, dimly aware of the reedy sound of the radio playing somewhere in the compound. I remember feeling shame, guilt, anger, fear . . . but perhaps most of all disbelief. How could this happen to me?

And even as I asked myself this question, a second Chinese man entered the room and raped me again.

I was returned to the dormitory building the following morning, where I found a spot on the floor and tried to make myself as small and inconspicuous as possible. I sensed the other girls talking about me and was grateful that my original clothes had been returned to me so I did not have to suffer the further indignity of being completely naked among them.

I was convinced that I could never go home now even if I wanted to. First, I had been witched. And now I had been shamed and ruined.

I was now a part of this world whether I liked it or not. Huddling against the back wall, I remained motionless all day and into the night, afraid that at any moment they would come for me again. But even when they did not, their absence seemed telling. It was as if I were an empty beer bottle that had been discarded or some other bit of useless garbage strewn about the compound.

I could not summon the energy to move until late into the night, and only then because I had to go to the bathroom. I stepped carefully over the bodies of sleeping girls and made my way across the front of the dormitory toward the outhouse. I walked quietly and turned my head away from the guard perched atop his platform.

I was bleeding and needed to clean myself. I broke off a small splinter of wood from the outhouse and scraped off the crusted blood on my legs as best as I could. But without water or toilet paper I did not do a very good job. The blood stains would serve as another reminder of this new world I lived in. It made me want to vomit.

Then I heard a commotion on the opposite side of the compound, followed by a girl's voice—a voice that was strained and pleading. Not daring to leave the outhouse, I pressed my face against the wall and peered out from between the wood slats. Alieu and a second man were dragging a girl in my direction. It was the tall girl that was brought with me to Ming's office the day before. She was completely naked.

Just as I thought they were headed directly to the outhouse, they turned and passed by me, moving toward the forest on the far side of the compound, where a small structure stood by itself. Looking like a thinner version of the outhouse, it rose above the surrounding tree stumps like a coffin standing on end. The gaps between its wood planks had been filled with something like dried mud, leaving just a narrow slot above the door as the only ventilation. It was completely exposed to the sun and the elements.

The girl pleaded with the men as they dragged her through the mud. By the time they reached the structure, her pleading had become less determined and more measured, as if she were praying. Alieu fiddled with a padlock on the door and placed the girl inside, locking the door behind her. As the men walked away, the girl let out a bloodcurdling scream that made me jump. Alieu paused but quickly turned and caught up with the other man, disappearing behind the buildings on the opposite side of the compound.

As I was shuffling back to my room, Alieu reappeared from among the buildings. Spotting me, he raised his hand and whistled. I froze and looked down as he approached, cursing myself for ever leaving the room.

But Alieu approached me in an easy manner, as if walking up to a friend on the street. He smiled, leaned his rifle against the dormitory wall, and took out a cigarette. Glancing at the narrow box, where the muffled sobs of the girl could still be heard, he said, "They call it a sweatbox." He told me that the girl would be there all night and throughout the following day. "Maybe even longer," he said darkly. "She will suffer greatly in there. It is very cruel." He looked at me as if to gauge my reaction, but I remained silent.

Alieu continued, telling me that the girl had tried to run away during the night, but they had found her very easily. He motioned toward the box. "That is her punishment. Mister Ming—he is not somebody to make angry at you." Alieu paused and studied me, squinting through the smoke from his cigarette. "You are suffering now, I know," he said. He told me that he had seen the same look many times before—every day, in fact—and suggested that I do what people said from now on. He said there was no going back and I should just obey. He pointed at me with his cigarette. "Do not fight, OK? These men will kill you. I have seen it with my own eyes. Your life before . . . it is finished now."

I considered his words for a moment before asking him where I was going. But he just shrugged and responded that he was not exactly sure. He said the others did not tell him such things because he was just a guard. However, he thought I would be sent very far away—perhaps even to a rich man overseas. "A collector," he told me. When I asked him what that meant, he entered into a long diatribe on the strange ways of rich men and how they liked to collect women from around the world. He clucked his tongue and looked off into the distance, as if trying to imagine himself what that might look like.

I silently studied Alieu. Despite everything that had happened to me, I could not help but like him, even wondering if we could have been friends under different circumstances. "Why are you with these men?" I asked. Alieu smiled and shifted his gaze down in an almost embarrassed manner, kicking at the ground with his foot. "All of us Africans, we are still . . ." His voice trailed off as he struggled to find the words, or maybe, I thought, because he had found the words but did not want to speak them. Finally, he shrugged again and said simply, "We must all survive."

Finishing his cigarette, Alieu slung the rifle across his shoulder and repeated his advice not to fight or run away. "You must listen to me or you will only suffer more," he said, before smiling weakly. As he walked away, he turned and added that I would be leaving in the morning, noting that the girl in the sweatbox was supposed to join me but now she would have to remain behind. "It will not go nicely for her," he said. "So you must accept what God has given you."

As I returned to my room, I wondered how God could possibly be any part of this.

6

ALIEU WAS AS GOOD AS HIS WORD, and I was loaded onto a truck the following morning. As I made my way across the muddy compound, I gazed at the sweatbox. It was a particularly humid day, and the structure stood eerily silent in the thick, dank air. The surrounding forest seemed even more sinister in the rippling heat, and I felt my head spin as beads of perspiration trickled down my forehead. I wondered if the girl in the box would even survive the morning. The box itself revealed nothing as it cooked in the blazing sun.

Riding in the back of the truck on that particular day also proved to be a grim business. As always, it was crammed with so many goods that I was forced to compete with my fellow passengers for the remaining space. Alieu took pity on us and jammed two sticks on either side of the door before closing and securing it to the bumper with some bits of rope, which allowed more air to flow through. Even so, I was drenched in sweat within minutes.

The next several days were a blur of rugged dirt roads interspersed with somber rest stops carved out of an increasingly thick junglelike environment. Two new men—both Chinese—took turns driving the truck. They were accompanied by an African man, who was relegated to sitting on the roof of the truck even though there was plenty of room in the cab. To my relief, all three men seemed disinterested in their human cargo beyond ensuring that we were alive and did not try to run away. But the environment itself discouraged any thought of escape; there was something sinister and primeval about the jungle that compelled everyone to stay close.

I kept to myself and made little attempt to reach out to the other girls. They were all new to me and spoke either French or a local language. The one girl who did speak English was so sick that she could barely utter a word. Most were transferred to another truck on the second day. On the third day, they picked up a new girl. And so it went.

The girl who joined us on day three spoke English and was able to tell me something about our general location. She said she was coming from Goma in the Democratic Republic of the Congo and believed we were still in that country near a town called Butembo. I was shocked to learn that the girl was not in the truck against her will. In fact, she claimed to have sold off the last of her goats to raise enough money for the ride. She told me that her husband had died of AIDS and she was now making her way to Juba in southern Sudan. She said her in-laws had blamed her for infecting her husband with the virus, accusing her of using witchcraft to kill him while managing herself to survive. But she denied the charge. "He was a wealthy man," she said. "So he had many girlfriends. But I was always faithful to him." After the funeral, her in-laws descended on the farm and took everything. She was forced to flee in the middle of the night with only a few goats. "I would have accepted an offer from my husband's younger brother to be his second wife," she said. "But he was scared away because of the witchcraft accusation." She leaned against the wall of the truck and sighed dejectedly. "So I am going home now."

All my life, I had heard similar stories of women whose husbands died and who had everything taken from them. I knew widows had little say over anything and few options available to them. So this girl's story was nothing new to me. Yet in some strange way, I almost envied her; at least she could go home—she had that choice. She did not realize what a gift that was.

But I was most interested in the fact that the girl knew our current location and general destination. The only thing I knew about southern Sudan was that it had been at war for a very long time, but the circumstances surrounding that conflict were a mystery to me. I asked if there were many rich men in Juba, wondering if it was where the man who "ordered" me came from. But the girl only laughed in response, adding that there were few rich people in her country after so many decades of war. "There is only suffering," she said. "And now hope."

After another long day of relatively uneventful driving, the girl told me that we had entered Uganda, and later that evening, we crossed into southern Sudan. In both instances, the border crossing was so unremarkable that I would never have known it had happened. Emphasizing that we were traveling the main roads rather than taking detours, my traveling companion speculated that the Chinese drivers had bribed the border officials to let them pass. That was why they did not inspect the truck or open the door to check for anything out of the ordinary.

Eventually, we pulled into a small compound situated on the banks of a massive river. It cut into the earth like a living, breathing thing, a massive surge of water that was unlike anything I had ever seen before. I could not help but feel a little unnerved by its awesome power; it made the ground rumble beneath my feet.

"This is the Nile," the girl said. "Juba is just on the other side."

———

I spent a restless night in a decrepit shell of a building next to the Nile. I felt the massive surge of water hum and pulse beneath the ground; the vibrations seemed to flow through my body and kept me awake for much of the night. When I finally did manage to sleep, I was awoken almost immediately and told that I would be leaving within the hour. I was shocked to discover that I would be traveling by bus on the next leg of my journey. Despite being an old, rickety clunker, the bus had windows, which meant that for the first time I would be able to see where we were going.

When I climbed aboard, I was immediately confronted with two dozen pairs of eyes that barely peeked out above the seat backs. The bus was packed with small boys, all of whom appeared much younger than me, some even as young as three or four. As I walked down the aisle to the only vacant seat in back, I could not help but notice something else about my fellow passengers: they each had a disability or some kind of handicap. Some boys were missing arms, some legs, while others had shriveled limbs or bodies bent in different positions, whether from birth or an accident I couldn't know. An assemblage of crutches and crude walking sticks poked out from above the seats like a small forest of flagless poles. I turned my head from side to side, meeting an array of wide-eyed stares with one of my own. I could never have imagined anything like this.

I took a seat next to a boy with one leg, the other ending in a dirty stump that barely stuck out from beneath his tattered shorts. He looked up and smiled. "Hello," he said pleasantly.

"Do you speak English?" I asked.

"Yes," he answered with another smile.

"Do you know where we are going?"

"Yes," the boy responded in his easy manner. "We are going to Nairobi. You do not know where you are going?"

Absorbing this new information, I convinced myself that Nairobi was my final destination. From what I knew, it was a large city with plenty of rich and powerful people. Surely, this was the home of the mysterious man who had ordered a young Himba woman from Namibia.

Turning to the boy, I asked, "Why are you going to Nairobi?"

"For a better life," the boy answered breezily. "In Juba, there is nothing for us." He swept his arm to indicate the other boys. "Our families do not want us, people do not want to see us. We are a nuisance. We survive on the streets. All of us are the same. But Kenyans are generous people and much better off. They will help children like us to have a better life."

"But where will you go?" I asked. "To a church?"

The boy shrugged and smiled. "I do not know. But any place is better than here."

Considering this for a moment, I asked the boy, "Were you born in southern Sudan?"

"Yes," he answered.

"Have you ever been out of southern Sudan before?"

"No."

"Do you have a passport?"

"What is that?" the boy asked.

Looking around the bus, it dawned on me that these boys were in the same world I was. The only difference was that they did not know it. The "better life" they dreamed about did not seem possible.

Suddenly, a flatbed truck with military markings drove into the compound and skidded to a halt in front of the bus. Two soldiers dressed in military fatigues sat in back, smoking cigarettes and carrying large, treacherous-looking guns. Three men dressed similarly emerged from the cab and walked into a nearby building. After several minutes, they emerged and approached the bus. Another man hurried after them; he was clearly agitated and seemed to be pleading with them about something. He only stopped when one of the soldiers shoved him backward and pointed his gun at him threateningly. As the new arrivals climbed aboard the bus, my initial reaction was to marvel at how extraordinarily tall they were. They shared other physical traits as well: high cheekbones with sharp, angular features and deeply set eyes. These men were clearly from the same tribe, I thought as I eyed their leader, whose military markings and general demeanor set him apart. To my dismay, the man, who was so tall that he was forced to bend forward to keep his head from smacking the roof of the bus, ignored the boys completely and focused his attention immediately on me. He had an intense, almost fierce look in his eyes. Towering above me, he flicked his wrist and motioned for me to rise. He appraised me for several moments before smiling coldly and saying, "You are now the property of the SPLA."

The SPLA, as I quickly found out, was the Sudan People's Liberation Army, the military wing of the Sudan People's Liberation Movement (SPLM), which in 2007 was in the midst of transitioning South Sudan from decades of civil war toward becoming the world's newest country. But as I would come to discover, the SPLA was anything but a formal, disciplined army. From my experience, at least, it was little more than an organized crime ring permeated by a ragtag outfit of illiterate street thugs.

For the next several months, my home was a small compound of tin shacks and burned-out buildings squeezed in among the shantytown neighborhoods of Juba. Together with hundreds of other women and children who passed through what was generally known as the Hay Compound, I had in fact become the property of the SPLA. More specifically, I was the property of a Major Deng, a shadowy figure who, as far as I could tell, was in charge of the compound. Major Deng stayed at the compound only one or two nights per week, however, and entrusted day-to-day operations to Kuur, the tall man who'd pulled me from the bus on the banks of the Nile.

During my time there, I came to discover that the Hay Compound was an extensive human trafficking ring made up almost entirely of children. It was a kind of sorting center and temporary storehouse for young boys and girls from across southern Sudan, who were kept there for a few weeks before being shipped to various places across East Africa. Upon arrival, they were divided into three groups: boys, girls, and children with a handicap, usually a missing limb or some other obvious physical disability, which the region provided in bulk. I had arrived at a time when Deng and Kuur were transitioning their activities from a focus on young boys to the other two groups. As a result, few *watoto wazima*—a Swahili term meaning "whole boys"— passed through the compound. Apparently, this was in direct contrast to just a few years earlier, when, during the civil war, they had been in high demand by the SPLA. At that time, and after just a few weeks of training, they were given guns and shipped to frontline units in the north. But with the signing of the Comprehensive Peace Agreement in 2005, the demand for pliable, easily manipulated child soldiers was significantly reduced. As a result, Major Deng was now in the business of young girls, who were always needed as domestic workers in Juba and other major cities around the region. He also began trading in children with disabilities—both boys and girls—who were sent off to Kenya by the busload. I heard him joke once that disabled boys were "recycled child soldiers" who had been sent north years before when they were watoto wazima.

After my initial encounter with the boys on the bus, I wondered why they were such a valuable commodity to Kuur and Deng. So I developed a rapport with the Kenyan woman whose job it was to oversee this particular group. She was an open, talkative individual who actually seemed to enjoy her "job," as she called it. Prior to coming to southern Sudan, she had been involved with the Kenyan side of things, so she had a good understanding of how the entire scheme played out. She not only was eager to tell me everything but also at times seemed to openly brag about her "many job responsibilities."

It turned out that the entire operation involving children with disabilities was a means of banking on sympathy. At some point, someone must have run the numbers and discovered that a child with a severe disability begging on the busy streets of Nairobi brought in much more money than a child without a disability. That was why disabled children were almost always linked to what the Kenyan woman referred to as the "begging industry."

Kuur and Deng sent busloads of these children from southern Sudan to East Africa's major cities. Along the way, they made frequent detours to supply regional hubs with their precious cargo. Immigration officials and other authorities received regular payoffs so the buses could cross international boundaries without trouble. Nairobi was the major port of call, mostly because of the amount of money that circulated there, but also because Kenyans were believed to be more compassionate. Put another way, they were easy marks. Once there, groups of children were stashed together in cramped houses located in the informal settlements that proliferated on the outskirts of the city. Each morning, they were transported to strategic locations in the city center under the control of handlers, who often posed as a relative or an employee of a church or nonprofit organization. Handlers came equipped with elaborate stories, false identification, and extensive connections with city council members, police, and even senior officials in the Kenyan government.

Depending on the location, each child earned anywhere between thirty and fifty US dollars each day. Typically, it took twelve to fifteen hours to collect that kind of money, especially if handlers took full advantage of the peak earning hours during the morning and evening commutes. Over the course of the day, each child remained in the same spot with little if any respite from Nairobi's scorching sun, not to mention the dust, exhaust fumes, and general filth of its busiest streets. In most cases, the handler hired someone—often an older street child—who watched over several disabled children from a safe distance, ensuring that their earnings were safe and nobody disrupted or interfered with their activities.

Few children were spared from the long hours and brutal work conditions. Handlers even "rented" the very youngest children to women who posed as their mothers, who in turn received a percentage of the daily haul. Phony mothers earned twice as much as they would begging on their own, which many did anyway.

Children were kept in line through a combination of threats and promises of a better life. But as far as I could tell, their lives in Nairobi were probably very similar to those they had left behind, only now any money they earned went to their handlers. The Kenyan woman described it as an ideal business model: the overhead required to maintain a begging operation was low, especially when compared to the daily profits, and she pointed out how the risks were minimal because the children did not speak the local language, did not know anybody, and were less likely to run away, given the nature of their disabilities. In fact, it was almost impossible for a child with a disability to disappear into Nairobi's street scene since survival required joining a gang, and they had little chance of doing that because membership required certain skills they lacked—fighting, the ability to run away from dangerous situations, and cultural affiliations, to name a few.

After learning these details, described to me by the Kenyan woman in her strangely cheerful manner, I thought it best to keep my distance from my new acquaintance. To me, she was a strange combination of ruthlessness, ignorance, and moral depravity. Initially, and because she seemed to walk around the Hay Compound with more freedom than the rest of us, I had thought I could somehow leverage my relationship with her to improve my situation. But now my gut told me she was a person who would quickly and easily betray me.

In addition to myself, about a dozen other girls were more or less permanent residents at the Hay Compound. Together, we were responsible for taking care of the children as they passed through, a task that was very difficult given the overall conditions at the compound. Food was scarce and usually consisted of a giant vat of porridge made from cornmeal, which was so watered down that it looked like a pale, yellowish soup. Hunger and sickness were so common among the children that most seemed to have resigned themselves to it. Individuals were frequently taken away because they were too sick or starving to move or be of much use. Some were near death. Exactly where they were taken was anybody's guess.

My job was to help take care of the youngest girls. Our group was housed together in a simple one-room structure made from cement blocks and a tin roof that leaked badly. Large pools of stagnant, muddy water accumulated on the cement floor where we slept. The building lacked electricity and running water, and every window was either shattered or stripped out completely, which allowed swarms of mosquitoes to lay waste to us each night. Sleep was next to impossible.

As far as the girls in my care, the experience of one ten-year-old girl named Achor was typical. She was a member of the Ngok Dinka, a subgroup of the much larger Dinka tribe, whose members lived in Abyei, a small scrap of land on the fringe of the Sahel, which straddled the proposed boundary between the North and South. Ownership of the region had long been disputed, and it was a particularly contentious part of the negotiations leading up to South Sudan's Comprehensive Peace Agreement. An agreement about Abyei was never reached, however, and the issue was left to a vaguely defined referendum process designated for some distant point in the future, which allowed the region to remain a no-man's-land where roving bands of soldiers and militia could raid and plunder at will. Among the Ngok Dinka, the most feared militia group was the Messiria, a nomadic Arab people backed by the government in

Khartoum who claimed Abyei as an important cattle grazing area during the dry season. The Messiria formed heavily armed, mounted raiding parties known as Murahaleen who regularly attacked Dinka villages, stealing cattle as well as children. Boys and girls were pressed into slavery in towns and villages throughout the North, a practice with a long history in the region and one that the civil war had only reinforced.

When the Murahaleen raided Achor's village early one morning, they killed many men, including her father, who was a minor chief among the Ngok Dinka. Then they rounded up all the cattle and children, including Achor, and drove them north before the SPLA could mount a counterattack. Over several grueling days, the Murahaleen drove a mixed herd of cows and children across the desert. They pushed them relentlessly, often striking the children with their sjamboks—long, stiff whips made from leather hide. At dusk on the third day, they finally came across a water hole, which was little more than an ankle-deep pond of brown muck. It was enough, however, and everyone—children and cows—rushed forward in a mad frenzy to drink.

Earlier in the day, Achor had become separated from her two sisters when the Murahaleen divided them into two groups. She was so desperate to rejoin them that she decided to hide herself among the cows, gradually working her way deeper into the herd as the animals spread out to drink. When she reached the opposite side of the water hole, she lay flat on her back and covered herself in mud and cow shit, just barely poking her head above the surface to breathe and keep a watchful eye on the Murahaleen. Once they began driving the animals forward, she was terrified that they might trample her. She began to pray, and by some miracle, the animals moved past her on either side. She allowed herself to emerge from the muck only when she saw the dust clouds disappear on the horizon.

Achor walked west toward the setting sun, hoping to meet up with the second group and be reunited with her sisters. She stumbled across the barren desert for days, stopping during the hottest part of the day to rest in the meager shade offered by thorn bushes and stark, skeleton-like trees. Eventually, she was picked up by an SPLA scouting party, who dropped her at a makeshift camp for IDPs—internally displaced people—where she was placed with a group of orphans destined for Juba. The group grew in size as they were moved through a series of IDP camps in the general direction of the capital city. After several weeks, they ended up at the Hay Compound. The soldiers told the children they would be reunited with their families, so Achor still held out hope that she would find her mother, who she believed had also escaped the Murahaleen. I knew the soldiers had lied; most girls who ended up at the compound were destined to work as domestic servants. But we were under strict orders to never tell the children their true fate.

Major Deng in particular seemed to love his role as a transporter of human bodies, and he made sure the children who passed through the Hay Compound did so as quickly as possible. He often bragged that he was able to ship his human cargo as far as Uganda, Kenya, Tanzania, and the Democratic Republic of the Congo. "We are an international business," he would say. "We are developing South Sudan." If he thought a group of children was at the compound for too long, he became angry and withheld food or doled out beatings with greater frequency and viciousness. Sometimes he beat the children for no reason at all, especially when he was drunk or smoking marijuana. He chewed khat almost constantly, a leafy plant and mild stimulant that was a favorite of long-distance truck drivers and soldiers. As for the children, he encouraged them to get high by sniffing rags doused with gasoline because it made them easier to manage. The practice had the added benefit of making them forget about their hunger, which saved both time and money. Most children came to the Hay Compound already addicted to huffing, so Deng was only too happy to support their habit. At any given time, at least half the children were unconscious or so high from huffing gasoline that they could barely speak or move. Deng was especially fussy when it came to his supply of gas rags and made certain there was always a large supply on hand.

In addition to caring for the younger children, the older, permanent girls—including myself—were expected to fulfill other duties, including serving as sex toys for all the soldiers and government officials who visited the Hay Compound. During my first week, before I really understood how things worked, I was raped by at least five different men. I cannot recall how many times I was forced to have sex during that time. I only knew that it became such a part of my daily routine that it was almost as if I stopped thinking or caring about it. At first, I tried to resist, but I was so badly beaten that I could barely walk the next day.

Eventually, a Congolese girl took pity on me and advised me to attach myself to one of the soldiers as his "wife." She told me that life would be much easier for me if I became someone's "wife," especially if he was higher up in the chain of command. By that point, I had noticed that some girls seemed to escape the worst of the beatings and rapes. Even as I thought about how to become a Hay Compound "wife," Major Deng himself told me that he would take me as one of his "wives." He thought it was a waste to let others "eat such a beautiful prize," as he put it, but after bringing me to the compound he had been called away, which had made it impossible for him to protect me. He was so angry with several of the lower-ranking soldiers who had raped me in his absence that he had them removed to a military outpost in some distant and particularly undesirable part of the country.

I knew that Major Deng's offer was not really an offer at all; I had little choice but to become one of his "wives." Even so, Deng went through the motions of actually asking me to be his "wife," towering above me menacingly and awaiting a response, as if daring me to refuse. The only effect it had was to make me feel complicit, as if I had agreed to sell myself to the man, which only increased the guilt and shame I felt in doing so, particularly when I was forced to witness the ongoing suffering of the temporary girls who cycled through the Hay Compound.

I soon realized that the horrors I had experienced during my brief time as a "temp," as they were called, were nothing compared to the experience of these girls. Temps bore the full impact of the sex parties that took place whenever the enigmatic Kuur visited the compound, which he always did with an entourage of high-ranking soldiers and government officials. These parties could last several days; it depended on the amount of Johnnie Walker whisky, Tusker beer, and other alcohol they brought in from Kenya. As the men became drunk, they treated the girls with increasing cruelty, commanding them to do different things, dragging them around like dolls, grabbing, pawing, and eventually raping them without a second thought. Temps were likely to be raped ten times a night; it was a free-for-all. But even when a party was not taking place, temps were raped on a daily basis by the low-level soldiers who hung around the compound. It did not matter if girls were bleeding and in obvious pain; the men raped them anyway. There were girls whose leg and back muscles were so sore that they could no longer stand. Some were unable to hold their urine. One girl who remained at the Hay Compound longer than most developed large boils around her private parts, which then became so rotted and infected that they were covered with maggots by the end. Even after they removed her from the compound, a group of drunken soldiers came to the compound looking for her. I am certain they would have raped her still.

Girls who tried to run away or broke the rules experienced additional suffering. When actual beatings were thought to be necessary, they were usually performed with a one-meter-long plastic pipe to the back of the legs. The beatings could be severe, leaving the victim with ugly bruises, huge welts, and in some cases open wounds. Sometimes, soldiers beat girls simply because they thought it was a good way to keep them in line. I once saw a drunken soldier try to make a girl eat crushed glass because he thought she had spoken out of turn. In most cases, however, rape itself was the preferred punishment. Troublemakers were simply gang-raped or raped more viciously, if that was even possible. One girl who was thought to be too proud was gang-raped in front of everyone and then "married" to "the ugliest man of all" as a way to humiliate her. It just went on and on.

It was hard to imagine how the high-ranking soldiers and government officials who filed through the compound could be in charge of anything; they seemed content to drink themselves into a stupor and flaunt their BMWs, expensive watches, and American dollars. On more than one occasion, they engaged in fights and impromptu wrestling matches with one another, reminding me of the foolish boys I had known in secondary school. Yet by attaching myself to Major Deng as his "wife," I was at least protected from the very worst of it. I knew

I had to do anything I could to survive. Otherwise, I would have been thrown to the baboons.

After six months at the Hay Compound, I resigned myself to the fact that I was there to stay. When Deng boasted of how he had brazenly stolen me from "another group" by plucking me from the bus, I realized that the compound had not been my intended destination. Nevertheless, I believed that my long journey had finally come to an end. For some reason, God had deemed that this should be my fate, and I began to think of my own suffering, like so many of the girls, as a necessary precursor to a more rewarding life to come. But neither my captors nor myself knew how determined that other group was to get me back.

———————

Over time, I was tasked with more duties at the Hay Compound. One of these involved visiting Juba's main marketplace—Konyo Konyo—to shop for the meager supplies needed to keep the children alive. Mostly, this included buying bags of cornmeal and filling jerricans with water supplied by Juba's water vendors, who provided the city's residents with the precious resource by pumping it from the Nile in large tanker trucks and selling it at designated water stations throughout the city. The water station at Konyo Konyo, like the market itself, was always a chaotic scene. Hundreds of women and children pushed and jostled one another as they jockeyed for position around the tanker trucks, each individual juggling as many plastic jerricans as she could possibly carry. Around them, the market spread outward in a sprawling, unscripted mass of makeshift stalls and shacks selling goods and produce brought in from all across East Africa. Throngs of people coursed through the narrow, garbage-strewn lanes like cattle, pressing together so tightly in places that it was difficult to even breathe. To me, it always felt like a powder keg ready to explode.

On one particularly rain-drenched day in August, I was sent to Konyo Konyo market to buy cornmeal. An SPLA soldier accompanied me, as well as a second man, named Simon. Simon hung around the Hay Compound doing odd jobs, but his abilities were limited—a childhood case of polio had so affected his legs that he was forced to get around on a set of makeshift crutches. It was said that Kuur tolerated him only because he was a distant relative.

As we slowly made our way around the market, Simon paused to haggle with different vendors. The soldier, who looked both bored and irritated, eventually wandered off. I assumed he was going to visit one of the market's many prostitutes; the soldiers prized the young girls from Ethiopia who worked at Konyo Konyo. Sometimes, if the girl was a new arrival or not tied to a particularly strong "host," a catchall term that included everyone from hard-core pimps to households that employed girls as domestic servants—in which case the girl often made money on the side by sleeping with men at the market—the soldiers would bring her back to the Hay Compound. She would remain there as an in-house girl until they tired of her and sold her off to another host. They referred to this practice as "testing the market."

Within minutes of the soldier's departure, two men appeared and quickly got into an intense exchange with Simon. Though they were speaking Arabic—a language I did not understand—I could tell they were arguing about me. As the conversation grew more heated, Simon glanced about nervously, seeming to search for the soldier or anyone else who could help him. But we were alone amid a sea of people. Suddenly, one man pulled out a knife and in a single, swift motion plunged it into Simon's stomach. He toppled over his crutches and into a vendor's stall, scattering several bowls of beans and groundnuts onto the muddy ground. A woman screamed, and the crowd, without even looking to see what was happening, immediately scattered in every direction. It was as if they had been through this before and knew that running was the best option. The two men grabbed me and began dragging me down the narrow lane.

Before we could get very far, however, a loud shout came from behind us, followed by a commotion as more market goers dove behind tables and sprinted between stalls. I turned and saw the SPLA soldier running toward us with his gun raised in the air. He shot off a quick burst as a warning. My captors forced their way through the panicked crowd, but as we were jostled about they loosened their grip on me. It was all I needed; I spotted an open lane and made a break for it. Bolting down the muddy track, I swerved between shacks, trying to run in a zigzag pattern to lose my abductors. More shots rang out. I thought they came from my right, but it was difficult to tell because the sharp bangs bounced off the tin shacks and echoed in every direction. Frantic, I emerged onto a main path and fought the crowd as it pushed against me. It was impossible to tell where I was among the maze of shacks; I could be going in circles and never know it.

When I turned a corner, I saw one of my abductors. It was the man who had stabbed Simon. He was tall—even by South Sudanese standards—and he immediately spotted me from above the sea of heads. He sprang forward with a sudden, almost shocking burst of speed, shoving people roughly to either side. I let out a sharp gasp and whirled about. As I fought the crowd once again, I remember flashing on people's faces: a wide-eyed woman with a remarkably calm baby peeking out above her shoulder, a gang of young boys laughing and shouting as they pushed their way forward, a female police officer grinning sheepishly. I tried to step over an old lady who had fallen to the ground, but I tripped and fell against a table stacked with baskets of fish. I fully expected to feel the hard clasp of hands grabbing me from behind or even the thrust of a knife in my back. Lifting my head, my eyes fell upon a fist-sized rock that had been placed on top of some old newspapers. I grabbed it, cut quickly behind the stall, and ran up another alley, spotting a major thoroughfare about twenty meters ahead. I felt a surge of hope and sprinted toward it.

Emerging onto a busy sidewalk, I turned and almost collided with one of my pursuers. He must have thought the chase was over, because he stepped forward in an almost casual manner. It was a mistake. With all my might, I swung my arm upward and smashed the rock into the side of the man's head. He cried out in pain, stumbled into the street, and bounced off the side of a taxi as it sped by. He twisted around violently and fell into the gutter. I dashed across the street, ignoring the blaring horns and screeching tires around me. On the opposite side, a high wrought-iron fence lined the street, forcing me to run parallel to the market. My only hope was to reach the end and find a side street that took me away from the tangled web of stalls and tin shacks. A voice cried out from behind me, but I dared not turn around. Had I really hurt the man with the rock or just stunned him? Stumbling forward now, I cursed the fence. Finally, I spotted the end just half a block away. *Freedom*, I thought. Gasping for air, I dashed ahead and turned the corner. The second man was waiting for me and drove his fist into my face. It was the last thing I remembered.

7

I awoke in the back of a speeding pickup truck. I sat up and blinked, trying to adjust my eyes to the harsh glare of the sun as it set across a vast landscape of rolling grassland. For a brief moment, I imagined myself back in Namibia; the wide-open skies and expansive vistas reminded me of the Kunene. The air was surprisingly cool, even comfortable; we were clearly nowhere near Juba and its thick, stifling humidity. I leaned against the back of the cab, cautiously feeling the side of my face. My left cheek was raw and swollen, and I felt a little nauseated, but otherwise I was not seriously hurt. As for the nausea, I thought it might be due in part to having lost a lot of weight over the past six months.

But there was also something else: I could feel a deep sickness coming on. It had been lingering for a week or so now, reluctant to emerge, as if my body had been waiting for the right moment to surrender after having survived for so long under such harsh conditions. And it was not just my body; it was my spirit as well, the very core of my being. I felt as if everything I had ever believed in—about myself, about my family, about life itself—were collapsing in upon itself. The nausea I felt was just the first sign of something more ominous, some impending shutdown. I worried that I was HIV positive or pregnant—perhaps both.

The past six months had been a nightmare: the deplorable conditions of the Hay Compound, the revolving door of sick and maimed children, the endless rapes and beatings by SPLA soldiers and others—the very men, in fact, who were lauded as bringing forth the "world's newest democracy," a popular phrase in the press and among the general public when it came to the almost uniformly optimistic discussions about

South Sudan's coming independence. But to me these were just words now, words used by men with power as they raped women and sold children into slavery. The next group of men who seized power would use the same words while doing the same things. For people like me, the only thing to do was to stay as far away from such men as possible. Unfortunately, once they got hold of you, it was almost impossible to escape. Each group ate a piece of you before passing you on to the next. In their world, it was either eat or be eaten.

I watched the sun dip below the horizon and reflected on everything that had happened to me, realizing that I must have turned seventeen at some point during my stay in South Sudan. I wondered if seventeen years would be all the time I would ever have as I fell into a deep sleep that felt more like a long descent into nothingness. It marked the beginning of the dream stage of my ordeal. The shutdown had begun.

———————

I lay in the sand beside my grandfather as he sat by the Holy Fire. I ran my fingers across his feet, tracing the rough topography of cord-like veins and broken fissures that ran across his leathered skin, and thought about all the paths those feet had walked, all the things they had allowed him to see and experience. The Old One sat silent and motionless, as he always did in my dreams, his blind eyes staring vacantly across the smoldering ashes of the Holy Fire. I knew what he was doing: he was listening to the conversations of the elephants, and for that he did not need his eyes; he required only his feet. They were planted firmly on the ground before him now, like a pair of magical amplifiers, attuned to the vibrations of the great beasts as they lumbered across the rolling plains of the Kunene.

I looked up into my grandfather's foggy eyes, the backs of my fingers still brushing idly against his cracked skin, and marveled at all the mysterious things the elephants must be saying. What were their discussions like? Did they talk about their day? Did they gossip and chitchat about trivial things the way people did? Did they argue? But I knew how my grandfather, who was never known to give precise answers to anything, could be particularly frustrating when it came to answering my questions about the elephants.

"They are speaking in elephant time," he often said. "It is the middle of a very old conversation. You would not understand." Sometimes he leaned back and sighed, saying, "The feet do not always get along with the head." He did not actually say these things in my dreamworld, though; they were simply memories of things he said. In the dreamworld, he was always silent.

So I continued to watch the Old One, trying to interpret his stony veneer, amazed at all the wonderful elephant secrets he must be privy to: each soft footfall a word, each plodding journey a conversation, the miles upon miles of rambling tracks a thousand books. They always walked with such careful deliberation, I thought. They must be choosing their words very carefully. "I will never understand a single elephant conversation in my lifetime," I said to myself in my dream. Even so, there was something ancient and familiar about their movements, and it gave me comfort.

———

I woke up feeling fuzzy, as if the thick tendrils of sleep were still wrapped around me. The dream was one I had had many times before. But now it seemed to take on added weight and significance—it was somehow more relevant. I could sense that change. But its true meaning remained a mystery.

I still lay in the back of the pickup truck, though it was parked now. I sat up and looked around: I was in a clearing surrounded by a thick stand of large thorn trees. It looked like another compound, the kind I had become familiar with prior to my long detour in southern Sudan. My observation was confirmed when I saw a delivery truck on the opposite side of the clearing with two girls standing beside it. *So I am back to this*, I thought, *this spider web of roads and rest stops.* I already knew the routine.

As I struggled to climb out of the truck, a man approached me and said, "Ah, the lost girl from Namibia." Standing in front of me, he appraised me in a manner that I had become all too familiar with by this point. He shook his head sadly and said, "These people from South Sudan, they are not developed. They just take and take. Now you are skinny and all used up."

For me, it was a confirmation of what I had already come to suspect: I was back in the hands of my initial abductors and had now resumed my journey to my original, intended destination, wherever that was.

I joined the two girls by the delivery truck and discovered that both spoke English. They told me they were from a small town in eastern Kenya. When I asked them about our current location, they said we were somewhere just north of Nairobi.

"So we are in Kenya now?" I asked.

"Yes," they answered in unison.

"Are we going to Nairobi?"

The girls looked at one another and laughed. "No," one responded. "We are going to Dubai." They explained that Dubai was somewhere in the Middle East, but neither was sure of its exact location. They were to begin work there as domestic servants, they said, adding excitedly that Dubai offered many opportunities to further their education as well. I listened coolly as they speculated about all the wonderful adventures they would have, including how the truck might be taking them to an airport. I wanted to tell them how foolish they sounded, but I did not have the energy. The nausea and dizziness were overpowering now, and I could sense a fever coming on, all of which made me feel like I was somehow caught in a dreamlike state. Everything was coming on like a flood now. I abruptly sat down in the dirt and hugged my knees—ignoring the astonished reactions of the girls—and fixed my gaze on a spot on the ground before me. I wondered if the elephants were guiding me toward death.

The next leg of my journey was a feverish blur. As I grew sicker, reality became interwoven with my dreams, which now stretched into the realm of hallucination, until it was difficult to tell whether I was even conscious or not. Most memories that I thought were real involved staring into the blackness of the truck or lying on the ground beside it at night, looking up at one girl or another who was kind enough to care for me. I recalled a few feeble efforts to give me food and water, but for the most part

I could not keep anything down. At one point, I thought I overheard a whispered discussion as to when I was going to die.

I found myself staring up at the Old One again. As before, his rigid gaze was fixed on the emptiness before him. But now his head was wreathed in a swirling mass of stars and planets. They whooshed about him in wrinkled eddies of perpetual motion, as if he had tapped into some primal state, some secret portal to another way of being. I looked down at his feet, which were planted firmly on the ground before him—the way they were when he was listening to the elephants—and realized that he had managed to tap into some higher level in his quest to understand them. He was far away now, I thought, traveling along a vast network of celestial elephant pathways that I could only dream about. When I looked up again, the elephants were pinwheeling across the starry sky above his head.

The back door of the truck was flung open to a blazing sun. I crawled to the entrance and gasped in shock, tears running down my cheeks as I blinked and marveled at the site before me: water everywhere, water that stretched beyond the horizon. I watched it swell and ripple from a deep blue to an intense emerald green, and I realized that it could only be the ocean that my brother Timo used to talk about. He was right, I thought, it was truly like a second sky between the first sky and the land.

The water contrasted sharply with a shimmering white beach, where a chaotic scene was taking place before me. Several hundred people were being herded into lines by men wielding large sticks. In front of each line, a long, open boat lay at anchor about twenty meters offshore. One group was already being driven toward their boat; men, women, and children waded cautiously into the water while juggling their belongings above their heads. Adults carried some children, while others were not so lucky and struggled to keep their heads above water. The men with sticks were not afraid to use them and routinely struck people to keep them moving forward. I was so weak that I had to be helped down to the beach by our driver and another man, who placed me at the end of the nearest line. I sat in the warm sand and watched the scene before me.

Our driver greeted several of the stick-wielding men in a familiar fashion. He conferred with them for several minutes, gesturing toward us before handing over a wad of money, though I did not recognize the currency. When one of the stick men approached us, I feared that he would beat us like everybody else. But he simply lit a cigarette and leered at us. He said something and smiled, revealing a mouth largely devoid of teeth, and proceeded to beat and yell at everybody around us. Why we were spared from the beatings was a mystery.

When it came time to board the boat, I held on to another girl and we carefully waded into the water together. I did not know how to swim, and in my weakened state I was petrified of fainting or losing my balance. Judging by the actions and expressions of everybody else, I was not alone in my fear. It took some time to fill each boat, but once full each would immediately pull anchor and speed straight out to sea.

When I reached my boat, I was hauled aboard like a fish and pushed forward. It was general pandemonium as the crew shouted at the frightened passengers and shoved us toward our seats. People tripped and fell over one another as the boat pitched violently. A woman who was simultaneously juggling a baby and several pieces of luggage almost fell overboard when she lost her footing. She dropped a large bag in the water and watched dejectedly as it floated away, joining other pieces of luggage that bobbed up and down beside the boat. The man in charge of seating packed us in as tightly as possible; I was placed next to an older woman who carried something wrapped in a long plastic bag that jabbed me in the ribs and forced me to lean slightly over the side. We were made to sit in an awkward squatting position; everybody was bent forward over their knees and practically balancing on their toes. My legs were already beginning to cramp.

By the time we got underway, there must have been around fifty passengers aboard. We were packed together so tightly that we had no choice but to endure our half-squatting positions. Every available space that was not taken up by a human body was crammed with small packages and bundles of personal goods, even after people were forced to ditch their largest items. The crew consisted of three men: the driver and his assistant, who sat in the stern, and a third man, who positioned himself on the bow. People tied shirts and towels around their heads in a feeble attempt to protect themselves from the sun and salt spray.

After only ten minutes, the driver slowed the boat to a crawl. I realized that he was waiting for something, which eventually appeared as a speck on the horizon but reached us within minutes. It was a boat similar in make to our own but only about half the size. It held five men in uniform, three of whom leveled AK-47s directly at us. Across the bow in faded black lettering were the words DJIBOUTI POLICE.

"We are the police of the Republic of Djibouti," announced a heavy-set man sitting in front. "You must pay the clearance tax when leaving the country or else go to jail." He held up a stubby finger. "One franc for each person." The crew members on our boat seemed to know the drill and immediately set upon the passengers, shouting at them to pass their money to the back of the boat. A fair amount of confusion ensued as people scrambled for money while the bowman, stepping awkwardly among us, made certain everybody paid their share. Several passengers had no money, which led to more slapping and kicking but with no real affect. To my relief, I escaped the beatings once again and was simply ignored.

Eventually, the money was passed back to the driver, who, in turn, gave it to the policeman. This touched off an argument that must have lasted twenty minutes and led to three separate head counts. The matter was finally resolved when additional money was added to the pot from a stash the driver kept hidden under his seat.

Satisfied, the Djibouti police allowed us to pass, and we set out once again. I covered my head with a stray plastic bag, securing it as well as I could, but I still felt myself getting burned by the sun, especially on my arms and the back of my neck. The salt spray made things even more uncomfortable, and I silently cursed each time the boat kicked up another wave that struck me full in the face. To make matters worse, the wind picked up throughout the afternoon, causing the boat to pitch and roll in long, nauseating undulations. As seasickness set in, passengers tried but frequently failed to vomit overboard. I thanked God that I had been given a seat on the side of the boat.

It turned out to be a particularly brutal leg of my journey. While I was completely exhausted throughout the boat ride, I found it difficult to sleep. I was still very sick, and the dizziness, which was almost constant, intensified every time I closed my eyes. The awkward squatting positions we were forced to sit in did not help matters; everybody simply had to grit their teeth and endure.

We drove all day and night, stopping only when the driver needed to switch jerricans of fuel, and once when a woman fell into the water as she was relieving herself over the side. If the driver had not literally run into her after reluctantly turning around, she may never have been found. When we finally managed to drag her back on board, she heaved up seawater in violent convulsions.

I struck up a conversation with the woman sitting beside me, who told me that she was from a small village in rural Somalia, where Al-Shabaab had established a strong presence. She described how the group had put a stranglehold on almost every aspect of daily life, even stoning to death several local women accused of adultery. Fearing for her life, she had fled to Mogadishu, only to discover that it was completely ravaged by fighting between Al-Shabaab and soldiers from the transitional government. Government forces were supported by well-armed troops from neighboring countries, this time as part of a "peacekeeping mission" backed by the African Union. After so many years of violence, Mogadishu was a wreck, and its weary residents viewed the two sides, each of which were sharply divided into a bewildering array of factions, with a mixture of disdain and jaded indifference. By 2007, the fighting had been going on for decades and people no longer viewed any group in a particularly positive light. The current crop of peacekeeping forces, most of whom were from Ethiopia, had lost all credibility when, in the name of ferreting out suspected Islamists, they indiscriminately shelled civilian neighborhoods and shot whole groups of neighborhood men on the spot.

The woman sighed and shook her head. "I would rather be killed by my own people," she said. "It is less shameful." She described how she had fled Mogadishu and spent several months moving from one makeshift camp to another before deciding to join her sister, who operated a textile shop in Dubai's central marketplace. The idea to try her luck in Dubai had come to her in a dream. Revealing a slight glimmer of hope, she told me how Somali women were leaving for the city every day. "Perhaps the stories are true," she speculated, "and Dubai is a place where a woman like myself can finally live in peace and even make a little money." She was silent for a few seconds before adding, "And I have faith in my dreams."

Interested in what she might have to say about my own dreams, I described the recurring images I had been having of my grandfather and the elephants.

"These are important things," the woman said very seriously, after listening carefully to my descriptions. "You should not take them lightly."

"But I do not understand the message," I responded. "I do not understand the elephants."

"Why do you think there is a meaning that you must discover?" the woman asked. As I considered the question, the woman continued, "My dear, dreams are not like gold that you dig up from the ground. They are what you make them to be. They are like this boat. The boat can go anywhere. If you are the driver of the boat, you decide where it will take you."

———

Later that night, the dreams came to me once again. But the restless, fitful nature of sleep made it impossible for me to find any coherence or meaning in them. My grandfather was nowhere to be found, and in his absence the elephants were an indecipherable presence on the horizon. But even at that distance, I could see that they were mingling among one another or else standing and swaying back and forth, as if deliberating exactly where to go. Maybe they did not know what to say, I thought, or perhaps they were debating the matter. Or, more likely, I simply could not understand them. I sat on a rock and carefully planted my feet on the ground, but I heard nothing.

———

We spotted land around noon the following day, a barren desert dune scape that hovered on the horizon like smoke. Its strange, almost mystical appearance reinforced for me what I had already come to realize during the crossing: we were no longer in Africa. It was a terrifying thought, but at that point I was just looking forward to being back on dry land.

We were still about a hundred meters offshore when the driver suddenly cut the engine. The crew huddled together in the stern and spoke to one another in hushed voices, every so often scanning the shoreline with troubled looks. For some reason, they seemed uncertain of what to do. The passengers grew increasingly restless and a low, troubled murmur rose from the boat.

Surveying the coastline myself, I saw nothing out of the ordinary at first. But after I allowed my eyes to adjust to the sun's glare, a group of men in long white robes materialized on the beach. After a few more minutes, I noticed that not only were they dressed similarly but also each carried a long black stick. "Are they carrying guns?" I asked the Somali woman beside me. But before she could answer, three loud pops echoed across the water. They seemed to be signaling the boat to come ashore.

The effect on the crew was just the opposite, however, and for reasons I never understood, they grew increasingly agitated. Without warning, they began tossing bags overboard. The passengers immediately erupted in protest, and a shouting match ensued as the boat pitched back and forth dangerously. The captain produced a handgun from somewhere and held it at his side while his nervous crew continued to fling bags into the sea. The sight of the gun was the only thing preventing the angry passengers from charging forward and overwhelming the crew.

And then one of the crew members pushed a passenger overboard. Whether it was an accident or not was hard to say. But it was an older woman who fell clumsily into the water with a loud splash. She thrashed about wildly with her arms—it was clear that she could not swim. Frozen in horror, people watched as she tried desperately to grab on to a large bag of clothes floating beside her. But the bag twirled about uselessly until the woman, after one final lunge, disappeared below the surface. In the clear water, I watched her shimmering yellow dress fade and finally flicker out of sight like a brilliant fish. In the chaos that followed, several more people either fell or were pushed overboard. Other passengers jumped into the water on their own and started swimming toward shore. I was desperate to join them but knew I would sink just as easily as the woman in the yellow dress. Waving his gun about wildly now, the captain shouted in broken English that people who could not swim should grab on to the floating luggage and kick their way to shore. But I could see that most passengers were just as terrified of the water as I was.

When a male passenger got into a shoving match with one of the crew members, the captain stepped forward and shot the man in the leg. He fell backward into the other passengers as a large bloodstain quickly spread down his pants. Again, there was a brief moment of shocked silence and time seemed to stop as everything came to a sudden, sharp standstill. Then, as if on cue, the passengers rushed the captain and crew in a single furious surge. Panicked, I stood up to move toward the bow, away from the free-for-all that was taking place directly behind me. But I was unsteady from my sickness, and my legs immediately cramped from being stuck in the same position all night, so I was already off balance when someone bumped into me. I heard one final gunshot against the general uproar as I fell overboard.

Several others must have fallen in around me, because I immediately became entangled in a frenzied, clawing mass of arms and legs. Kicking and punching wildly at the bodies around me, I struggled to keep my head above water. I managed to break free and give myself some space, but the battle to stay afloat was a losing one. In a final act of desperation, I lunged upward with one arm and, inhaling a mouthful of water, just managed to grab on to a length of rope that tied two large plastic bags together. I hauled myself up until my head popped out between the bags. Gagging and heaving up salt water, I slowly worked hand over hand along the rope until I managed to drag my upper body above the waterline. As it turned out, the rope was just loose enough to create a perfect space between the two bags, allowing me to work myself into a surprisingly stable position by tucking a bag under each armpit.

The boat was behind me now, but I dared not go back or turn around. The surrounding water churned with the frantic sounds of drowning, desperate people. I quickly decided that the only way to survive the pandemonium was to push forward. The shock of falling into the water had revived me, and I kicked my way toward shore, frantically at first but then in a more controlled, purposeful manner. It seemed to take hours, but slowly, bit by bit, I made my way toward the sliver of white beach. When I finally felt the soft grit of sand beneath my feet, a sudden rush of relief overcame me, and I crawled on my hands and knees until I collapsed on the beach. I must have lost consciousness momentarily, because when I opened my eyes, it took me several seconds to remember where I was. Lifting my head, I realized that only a handful of passengers had made it to shore; most had either drowned or remained on the boat, which bobbed listlessly offshore in the same general location. It looked like the passengers had taken control; they were plucking bags out of the water and hauling them back on board. I found myself hoping they had killed the crew.

Two men in white robes had to carry me down the beach, eventually depositing me with a small group of others who had also made it to shore. The passengers who remained on the boat slowly made their way in and joined us. Some individuals could barely move after being forced to sit in the same squatting position all night. Others were crying or looked as if they might be in shock. Overall, they were noticeably fewer in number than when we had set out. As for the crew, they were nowhere to be found. I never learned what happened to them or why they suddenly panicked at the end. The men in white robes did not ask or seem to care.

They marched us inland over a series of small dunes. I was still too weak to stand and so had to be carried by several men. They laid me in a blanket to make their job easier. After cresting the final dune, we came upon a natural spring surrounded by a cluster of tall trees and grass. Several large trucks were parked under the trees and, beside them, more men with guns sat about. They watched silently as the exhausted passengers straggled in. I was placed on the ground near one of the trucks.

A man with a neatly trimmed coal-black beard walked up to me and asked, "Where are you from?" I stared blankly up at him, uncertain of how to respond. I mumbled something about arriving on a boat from some far-off place.

The man scowled down at me. "No, no, no," he said. "I mean what is your home country?"

When I told him Namibia, I was surprised to see the man break into a wide smile and exclaim "Ah, good!" He then had me carried over to a small group of passengers who were kept separate from the others. It included two other girls and a dozen small boys who must have arrived on an earlier boat. The boys clustered together in a jittery little pack, glancing this way and that with uncertain faces.

Despite everything, I still puzzled over the man's reaction. It was hard to believe that, in the midst of all this chaos, there existed some underlying order, enough at least for someone to be expecting me and know where I was going. It reminded me of the invisible network of trails that connected one water hole to another in the Kunene. They may have been impossible for outsiders to see, but to each and every Himba, they were as plain as any paved road.

Once separated from the other passengers, our group was left alone. We soon discovered how lucky we were. The men in charge, whoever they were, set upon the second group, dividing them further into those who had money and those who did not. Those with no money did not fare well. The men had mobile phones, and from what I could figure out, they made each person call their contacts in the new country to collect additional money. One individual after another wept into the phone as they pleaded with friends or family members on the other end of the line. Those who were not able to call someone or were unsuccessful in their efforts to collect money were beaten. At this point, I was immune to the violence. I fell into a deep sleep.

―――――――

I was riding in a donkey cart through the Namibian veld. The rush of air on my face was warm but pleasant, and when I tilted my head back and looked up, I saw that it was night. The stars massed in cloudy streaks across a brilliant, midnight-blue sky. All around me the tall grass shimmered in the darkened glow, fluttering in sheets and waves as the wind swirled across the tops.

I was sitting beside my grandfather, who was staring straight ahead with his usual stony visage. He gripped the reins with one hand and held a whip with the other, bringing it down with a sharp crack in regular intervals, driving the donkeys faster and faster across the sea of grass. Astounded, I wondered how he was able to see where we were going. Yet he drove us on zealously, whipping the animals with a thunderous purpose and propelling our tiny cart into the night.

And then I felt an overwhelming presence behind us. Turning to look over my shoulder, I saw that we were spearheading a surging army of wild, trumpeting elephants. They stampeded forward as one, leaving in their wake a solid wall of dust and flying grass that spiraled above us like an angry storm cloud. There must have been thousands, I thought, as I turned back and gripped the wooden bench seat with excitement and anticipation. A feeling of euphoria swept over me and I laughed delightedly into the oncoming night. As the elephants bounded like gazelles on either side of us, I looked up at the Old One and was not afraid.

Early the next morning, I was awoken by the general commotion of people being loaded onto trucks. My group was loaded together into one of the smallest trucks. Initially, the ride was rough, and I prepared myself for another long, uncomfortable day, but we soon linked up with a paved road, and the ride became as smooth as any I had experienced up to that point.

I would not even have remembered this particular leg of my journey if not for one notable event the first night. I was jolted awake as the truck pulled off to the side of the road. After the passengers were allowed to clamber out and relieve themselves, the guards herded the group of boys to the front of the truck, and from out of nowhere, three men on horseback materialized out of the desert. They produced a long rope and tethered the boys together by looping it around their necks, then tied off the end to one of the horses. After concluding some business with the driver, the mysterious riders climbed back on their horses and slowly rode off into the night. As the boys trailed silently behind, pulled along by the rope, the last boy turned questioningly toward me and the other girls. But all we could do was stare dumbly back. It was as if their footfalls were aimless and muted, I thought, as I made a conscious effort to apply my dreams to what was happening around me. Their stories were already finished.

Two days later, the truck door was flung open for the last time to reveal an old woman dressed in a long black robe and headscarf. She stood in the middle of a large, empty courtyard framed by high cement walls topped with large metal spikes. Peering into the truck with sharp eyes set against an angular, weathered face, she said something in a language nobody seemed to understand. Scowling in frustration, she then barked, "Who speaks English?"

We turned toward one another for a few seconds before I stepped forward from the shadows. "I do," I answered.

The old woman slowly looked me over from head to toe. "Where are you from?" she asked.

"I come from Namibia," I answered. "That is my home country. My name is Tupa."

The old woman's eyes widened. "Ah," she exclaimed. "Our Namibia girl." She pronounced "Namibia" slowly and with a funny emphasis on the first syllable, revealing how little she knew about my country, other than the fact that she was waiting for a girl from there.

The old woman rummaged around in the folds of her robe before drawing out a piece of paper. She studied it and glanced at me several times before scowling again and thrusting it toward me. It was a photograph of a young Himba girl dressed in traditional garb, bare breasted and covered in the red ocher mix I knew all too well. I had seen hundreds of such images before; almost every travel magazine, brochure, or commercial advertisement related to Namibia had a photograph like it.

"Is that you?" The old woman asked. "Is that your . . . tribe? Your people?"

"It is a Himba woman from my tribe, yes," I said.

The old woman looked me over again. Finally, she said, "Good. He has been waiting for you and will be pleased to know that you have arrived."

While I had no idea who "he" was, I could not help but feel a sense of relief that my journey might finally be over.

Motioning for me to climb down from the truck, the old woman asked me, "Do you know where you are?"

"No."

"You are in Dubai," she said. "This is your new home."

8

FOR SEVERAL DAYS, I was confined to the servants' quarters at the back of the complex. Servants were housed in a narrow, windowless building partitioned into tiny rooms that were barely big enough to hold a cot or, in my case, a thin, badly worn foam mattress deposited on the cement floor. During the day, the rooms got so hot that they were unbearable, and it was better to sit in the narrow alleyway between the main house and the garage, where the high walls created an almost constant shade and even a slight wind tunnel effect if you were lucky. During their daily thirty-minute breaks, staff members often napped or ate here since they were not allowed to spend their breaks in the air-conditioned main house.

"You are much too skinny," Madam Dua told me when I was finally brought before her again. The old lady's eyes narrowed and roamed over my body with a look of disgust. "I cannot have you looking so sick and pathetic. I hope you did not get AIDS from some savage in Sudan. If you are HIV positive or pregnant, he will never have you. You must focus on eating and gaining weight. Meanwhile, we must test you." For now, Madam Dua commanded, I was not to work or even "move around with too much energy." Instead, I was to do nothing other than sit, sleep, and eat several large meals each day, which consisted mostly of big chunks of red meat and piles of pasta. I was only too happy to comply.

Sitting in the alleyway by myself each day, I had time to reflect on everything that had happened to me. I had been taken against my will, placed under a curse by a powerful witch doctor, raped, appraised, sold, and thrown in the back of a truck and shipped to some distant part of the world. And for what? To sit in an alleyway waiting to become somebody's servant? It did not make sense to me. Did Himba women have a reputation for making good servants in Dubai? Why me? There were just so many unanswered questions.

I wondered if any of it even mattered any longer. After all, I was ruined now—spoiled and shamed—a common whore with little use or value to my family or others. Even if I did manage to return home some-day, how could I face my people? And then there was the curse I was under, which made it all but impossible anyway. I could feel it working inside of me, a kind of heaviness that spread throughout my body like a disease. Sometimes, I was convinced that others could see it, too, as they talked about me behind my back. I imagined them pitying me like some doomed creature with no hope or future.

My thoughts also turned to my father. Why had he not done more to prevent his only daughter from being taken? When I considered his actions on that day in Angola, I was filled with so much disappointment and anger that it was difficult to dwell on. I even began to wonder if my father and uncle had arranged for my abduction beforehand. Maybe they were promised a lot of money for me. Maybe they had raised me for this very purpose. Why else would my father so easily agree to give me away? It made me feel hollow inside. Everything and everybody I had ever known or trusted had deserted me.

A few days after my arrival, another servant—a strikingly beautiful girl from Ethiopia—came to my room and invited me to share her dinner. "You must eat," she said, looking at me with concern. "You eat when the food is ready and speak when the time is right. That is what we say where I am from." She flashed a big, open smile and brought me to her room, which contained an actual cot, where we could sit and eat together.

Her name was Almaz, and she was from a small town on the outskirts of Addis Ababa. She told me that when her husband had died in a traffic accident, she had been left to fend for herself and their two children. She had answered an ad in the newspaper calling for domestic workers in Dubai that promised salaries much greater than anything she could hope for in Ethiopia. "Many women from my country come here to work," she said. "It is very common, and there are always advertisements in the paper for maids and nannies. Just imagine: they offer maids one hundred fifty dollars a month here, while in Ethiopia the same job will only pay ten dollars a month, if you are lucky enough to get it." The main reason she took the job, she explained, was to send money home to help her children survive.

I was incredulous. "You came here on your own? You were not forced?"

"Yes," Almaz answered. "But it is not what I expected." She described how the recruiting agency had flown her to Dubai with five other women. When they arrived at the airport, the women were led to a room where their passports and all of their belongings were taken. Then they were made to sign papers that they were unable to read or understand because they were written in Arabic. Following that, they were delivered to their respective "sponsors." In Almaz's case, she discovered that her salary was to be $20 per month rather than the $150 promised to her, because, as the recruiting agency informed her, it would be docking money from her paycheck to reimburse itself for her flight to Dubai.

"I think that is what those papers I signed at the airport were all about," she told me. "So now I am here, and it will take me many years to pay my debt back. But twenty dollars a month is still good, and I manage to send most of it home to my children." She shrugged her shoulders and said, "So, here I am." Snatching some food from her plate with a piece of folded bread, she exclaimed, "Ech. They do not even give us a knife, these stupid people."

Almaz gave me a more thorough tour of the servants' quarters, showing me the shower and toilet area, which was a small room shared by everyone; the laundry and ironing area; a supply room; the gardener's shack; and a few other outbuildings. As we walked around the compound together, Almaz pointed to the walls surrounding us. "Everything is high walls here, always walls, everywhere walls. Everybody is separated by walls. You will see."

In fact, I had already taken note of the many walls and their menacing spikes. "Do they have many criminals here?" I asked, as I ran my hand along the rough cement.

"No, not here in these neighborhoods," Almaz responded. "These Arabs are funny people—very secretive. But I think these walls are for keeping us in. We are not allowed to go out. It is only work for us."

"Are we prisoners, then?" I asked.

Almaz considered this for a few seconds. "Yes, maybe. We are servants—invisible servants—but we suffer like prisoners. So yes, maybe." She shrugged her shoulders. "But we suffer so our children can have better lives."

"I do not have children," I said.

Almaz smiled. "Ah. Well, maybe one day you will."

It seemed pointless to me—to have children and never see them in order to work like this. No, I thought, I was not ready to accept that. If I ever had children, I would never allow myself to be separated from them. I would not be like my father.

Almaz explained that the family we worked for was rich and powerful—even by Dubai standards. The man held a very high position in a government ministry and also partnered with his eldest son in a private business venture. She thought it might involve real estate development, but she was not certain. The man's wife did not work but kept busy by entertaining guests and doing a lot of shopping. Otherwise, she preoccupied herself by supervising staff, inspecting their work, and generally hounding them. "She is not a good person," was all that Almaz would say, shaking her head. In addition to the eldest son, who lived on his own, the couple had three other children—another son and two daughters—who still lived at home. The man's father, who was old and required almost constant care and attention, also lived at home.

The family had many domestic staff members, including eight full-time individuals who lived in the servants' quarters and two part-timers who stayed elsewhere but helped out with special occasions like parties. All were women with the exception of one man, who worked as a gardener and groundskeeper. "These people are lazy," Almaz said in response to my astonishment at the large number of servants. She added that the Arabs considered it shameful to do domestic work. "You see, they are very much full of pride. It is a sign of wealth and importance for one family to have many servants; it tells everybody that they are powerful." She explained that it was considered fashionable in Dubai to have servants from all over the world, ticking them off on her fingers as she listed them: "Two from the Philippines, three from Indonesia, two from Sri Lanka, one from Pakistan, and now two from Africa." She rolled her eyes and laughed incredulously. "It is a collection. And since we are Africans, we are at the bottom. We have the worst jobs and are paid the least. You will see what I mean as you begin your duties."

I liked Almaz's directness and listened carefully to everything she told me. It was good to finally know what was happening around me, rather than to have everything simply unfold before my eyes. I appreciated having such insight now more than ever.

"And you must know about Madam Dua," Almaz continued. "She is the manager of the house. Maybe you have seen her already—she is the very old lady who dresses in the long black sheet."

"Yes," I said, "she was the first to . . ." I was about to say she was the first person to "greet" me, but that was not the right word. ". . . see me," I finally said.

"She is an old cow," Almaz said bluntly. "But she is a distant relative of the family, so she can do as she pleases. Perhaps soon God will judge her for all her evils." She made the sign of the cross and spit on the ground. "A very bad woman," she added. "She is our supervisor."

I told Almaz about meeting with Madam Dua upon my arrival and how the old woman had showed me a photograph of a Himba woman. "Why are they interested in my tribe?" I asked.

Almaz bit her lip and turned away. "This is another matter," she said, so faintly that it was practically a whisper. "It is about someone who is away on business now. It is not something you need to worry about at this time." She did not elaborate further.

After a couple of weeks of doing nothing, during which time I managed to gain most of my weight back, Madam Dua finally summoned me once again. We met in a small room off the kitchen. It was the first time I had been in the main house, and the air conditioning offered a nice respite from the relentless heat. Madam Dua wore the same black dress and headscarf, which framed her bony, lined face and accentuated its timeworn appearance.

"You are a lucky girl," the old lady said sharply, without looking up from some papers she was reading. "Your tests show that you do not have HIV and you are not pregnant. If you were, I would have turned you over to the police as an illegal." I could hardly believe the good news;

I had been sure that, at the very least, I was HIV positive after my long ordeal in southern Sudan. Though I had pushed it to the back of my mind, I was still living each day with the shadow of AIDS hanging over me. So now, for the first time, I felt like I could see a small glimmer of hope in the distance. Once again, the actions I took while living under Kuur's authority had paid off. *Don't just wait for death*, I thought. *Always try to do something, try to find some room to maneuver. It just might work.*

Now Madam Dua looked up from her papers. She pointed her bony chin at me and immediately launched into a long list of job duties I would be expected to do each day: "You will begin each day at six o'clock AM. You will wash the cars first, then assist the gardener with watering the plants, both inside and outside; then you will wash and iron the clothes until breakfast is finished; then you will wash the dishes; then you will finish with the laundry; then you will clean the house until two o'clock PM, when you are allowed to have a thirty-minute break; then you will clean the dishes from lunch; then you will return to your house-cleaning duties. After dinner, you will clear the dishes. You will also assist the Ethiopian with the care of Master Hammad—the old man—who requires a bath every evening. You are also responsible for keeping the servants' quarters clean and organized. You will rake the grounds in the evenings. Sometimes you will be required to help with the cooking, but this is not the usual job of our Africans. You will be working with the Ethiopian, and she will show you how each of these jobs is to be done. You will learn the details from her as you work."

I remained silent, relieved to know that I would be working with Almaz, "the Ethiopian," as Madam Dua described her. The old lady spoke so quickly that it was difficult to remember everything she said. She did not elaborate or leave any impression that I should ask questions or even speak, talking at me with such rigid intensity that it felt like a chicken was pecking at my ears.

Following the explanation of my job duties, Madam Dua then turned to the rules of the house: "You are not allowed to leave this house without permission, and you are not allowed to go anywhere by yourself. You are not allowed to communicate with anybody outside of the house. While you are working in the house, you do not speak unless you are first spoken to, especially with the family members. You do not look them in the eyes—you look down at the floor. You call the women 'madam' and the men 'master.' They are your *kafeels*—your sponsors—and you must always respect them, because you work for them and because they are a respected family in Dubai. They are much higher than most people. You cannot understand this, but you must always show them the proper respect. As for you, you are *khaddamah*—the help."

Madam Dua paused, presumably to catch her breath, before outlining additional rules: "While you are working in the house, you must never sit on the furniture or lie down in the beds. You must always wear the appropriate clothes that we provide you. The Ethiopian will see to it. You must keep your hair pulled back in a scarf. Your appearance and clothes must always be kept neat and clean. You must not smell, and you must shower every morning. And you must never become pregnant. The punishment for sexual relations is very hard. Do you understand this?"

I nodded consent, but Madam Dua did not appear to notice. "You are on a probation period of three months to evaluate your performance and ensure that you are a suitable fit. During this time you will not be paid. If we decide to keep you after three months, then we will pay you the appropriate amount. But even then, for the next several years most of your paycheck will be deducted to pay back your recruiter and the costs of bringing you here."

At this point, Madam Dua gave a long explanation of something called the *kafala*—sponsorship system. And though I did not understand any of it or why it was being explained to me, eventually—and with Almaz's help—I pieced together its fundamental tenets. I discovered that maids, nannies, and other domestic workers in Dubai—and the United Arab Emirates in general—were considered part of this mysterious kafala system. In the end, it meant that they did not have access to any benefits or rights under national labor laws. Instead, they were defined as migrants who fell squarely under the realm of the Ministry of Interior, which rarely interfered in matters considered to be part of a private household. As far as the government was concerned, household or family disputes were just that, and not something the government wanted to get involved in. As migrants, domestic workers were subject to a set of immigration laws that were put in place to protect their employers, who, under the kafala system, also were their sponsors. In the end, individual households had complete and total control over their servants and could do with them as they pleased.

At the time, however, I was simply confused. I could not understand why Madam Dua was talking about me as if I were an employee beginning a new job, rather than somebody who had been kidnapped and enslaved. Did she even know how I had come to be here? Or was this just a clever way to disguise everything?

But the old lady left little doubt about the answers to these questions when she produced an Ethiopian passport and said, "This is your passport." Opening it, she showed me a photo of myself that had been taken at the camp in the DRC right before I was raped by Ming. I had never owned or even seen a passport before, not even from my own country. Looking at the phony document before me now, I began to understand how extensive the connections were when it came to my abduction; the network extended from Dubai all the way back to Namibia. I could hardly believe it.

"I will keep this," Madam Dua continued, referring to the passport, as if it were of any real value to me. "So you must obey the rules. If you do not, there can be very big problems for you. In Dubai, you go to prison for a very long time if you fail to pay your debt. And you have signed a work contract with us. It is here." She extended a bony finger to a document on the table before her. It was written in Arabic. "You have already signed it," Madam Dua said. "It is the same signature as the one on your passport. It is already done."

The old lady sat back and eyed me curiously. "I think you also know that you are under a very strong curse . . . yes?" I gave a small start, which prompted a triumphant sneer from Madam Dua. She continued, "And your family is also part of that curse. You do not want to do anything that would put them in danger. It would be very bad for them. You would be killing them. It has happened many times before with this curse. You cannot escape it."

I did not respond. Even so, Madam Dua seemed satisfied with my reaction; it was impossible to hide my distress, especially when I was reminded of the danger my family was in. It made me angry to think how easily this old woman could strike me where I was most vulnerable.

But Madam Dua was not finished, and she proceeded to spread a series of photographs on the table. They were photos of the Chinese man raping me. Somebody had taken them without my knowledge; it was hard to remember the events of that night, in part because so many other horrible things had happened since then. Unable and unwilling to even look at them now, I turned my head away. "You understand that I have these photographs now," said the old lady. "They are very shameful, yes? You do not want your family to see these, do you? And your friends? Everybody you know? I think that would be very bad for you. Very bad. I think you understand me. These will be given to everybody you know if you do not obey the rules."

Madam Dua paused again, letting everything sink in, scrutinizing me with her intense, penetrating eyes. She radiated an energy that was almost palpable, like a coiled snake ready to strike. "Now," she said, "let us talk about this." She placed one more photo on the table; it was the same magazine photo she had shown me before, the one of a Himba woman in traditional dress. "So you are from this tribe, yes?" she asked.

"Yes," I answered.

"What do you call yourselves?"

"I am from the Himba tribe. We are from Namibia."

"Yes, good," said Madam Dua. "Himba." She seemed to recognize the name as meaningful in some way. "And this . . . costume . . . you know how to make this? If you are provided with the materials?"

I hesitated, unsure of how to respond. Beyond the strangeness of the question itself, I had no idea if the materials were available in this part of the world. And even if they were, I had not worn traditional clothes since I was a little girl and did not really know how to make them.

But Madam Dua did not seem to think a response was necessary. She waved her hand dismissively and said, "You will be provided with materials, and the Ethiopian will help you. Do you understand everything that I have said to you here today?"

I said yes, though in reality I understood very little.

"Good," Madam Dua said. "You can go, then. You begin work tonight. Find the Ethiopian. She will tell you what to do."

As I stepped out, Madam Dua called after me. "Wait. You understand that if anybody asks you if you are a virgin, you should say yes. Only I am to know about this." She waved her hand over the photographs in front of her with a disgusted look. "And you," she added ominously.

———————

Over the next two weeks, I settled in to my new life, which consisted of little beyond sleep and work. I worked fifteen hours each day, waking up at 5:30 AM to begin washing the family's four cars by 6:00 AM, a job that took a full ninety minutes to complete to Madam Dua's satisfaction. Next, I helped the gardener—a quiet man from Pakistan—to water plants, rake the grounds, and generally help with the landscaping. The bulk of my day, however, was taken up with the endless task of cleaning the interior of the house, which was kept in such a pristine state that it approached sterility. And while cleaning the house, I was expected to find time to wash and iron clothes. On occasion, I was enlisted to work in the kitchen, especially if there was a dinner party or some other event where help was needed. Generally, however, the Sri Lankan laborers worked in the kitchen; it was not considered proper or desirable to have "the Africans" involved with food preparation.

Apparently, caring for the elderly was something that did fall within the realm of the Africans, since Almaz and I were given the particularly dreary job of looking after Master Hammad, who turned out to be the very old, bedridden father of Dr. Kassab. Each day, we had to feed and wash him, clean his bedpan, change his clothes and sheets, move him into various positions to prevent bedsores, and put him in his wheelchair and take him outside for thirty minutes during the evenings when it was cooler. Waiting on him was a thankless job made more difficult and irritating by the fact that the old man spoke only Arabic, and only then in a mumbled slur. For the most part, he lived a lonely, miserable life.

The entire household operated on a set of simple and very conspicuous racial assumptions. Jobs were clearly defined in terms of what Madam Dua and the family assumed were the inherent skill sets and capabilities of different races, ethnicities, or national identities. To them, Pakistani men made good landscapers, Filipino women were good with children and made acceptable personal servants, Sri Lankans were good in the kitchen, and Africans—who occupied the lowest rung on the ladder in terms of pay and perceived ability—were tasked with cleaning and assisting others when needed.

Madam Dua articulated these beliefs on a daily basis, mostly when criticizing different staff members. For example, the Filipinos were conniving, the Sri Lankans were stupid and lazy, and the Africans were a combination of all these traits and more, she said. One day, Madam Dua pulled out a local newspaper and showed me the Help Wanted section. "You see," she said, "whenever there is a servant wanted for a cleaning position, they advertise for a woman from Africa. It is known that is all you can do." I was not sure whether to be more astonished at the blatancy of Madam Dua's racism or the fact that she was correct in that every cleaning position sought an "African female" or sometimes "Ethiopian female or approximate."

Madam Dua was fond of reading newspaper articles to the staff, especially if they were about the so-called foreigner problem, an issue that—according to her, anyway—was popular among Emirati, the citizens of the United Arab Emirates. She was particularly fond of opinion pieces that focused on how the many foreigners in the UAE were undermining Emirati society and culture. Domestic servants—because they were foreign, mostly female, and based inside the household itself—represented a particularly potent combination of risks. According to the articles Madam Dua read, they were condemned for a whole host of things, including posing a threat to Islamic norms, being a bad influence on children, using witchcraft on their employers, poisoning their sponsors' food, and generally being walking, talking health hazards. In the same vein, the old lady once posted a dispatch from the Dubai police highlighting things "to watch out for" when monitoring domestic servants, which involved a host of potentially strange behaviors and drastic mood swings.

As for Dr. Kassab, I rarely saw him; he often did not come home until late, when I had already finished my duties inside the main house. When I did see him, it was because he was visiting his father, Master

Hammad. In fact, he was the only member of the family who dropped in on the old man for any length of time, often reading to him in Arabic from a tattered, ancient-looking book, which, according to Almaz, was a book of poems. In general, he was a quiet, even gentle man who took very little notice of me or any of the servants; in fact, I never once saw him speak to any of us, even the two Filipino women, who spent the most time around the family. It was difficult to imagine him as the person who "special ordered" me. But if it was not him, then who? It was definitely not his daughters, who were both very young. His teenage son was rarely home himself and seemed interested only in his girlfriend and his Humvee. Even when he complained that I had done a poor job cleaning his giant car, which happened on several occasions during the first few weeks, he informed Madam Dua, who would then relay that message to me, usually accompanied by a significant amount of yelling and slapping.

Other than Madam Dua, the only family member who interacted with the servants—especially the "lower" servants like Almaz and me—was Dr. Kassab's wife. Madam Kassab was a physical contrast to Madam Dua: she was plump and doughy with soft, creamy skin and a youthful, almost childlike face. She ran the household with a nervous, high-strung energy. While having none of the shrewdness or cold, calculating abilities of Madam Dua, Madam Kassab did share her enthusiasm for belittling the servants. She barely controlled her hyperanxiety and could erupt at any moment into violent screaming fits, which for the most part were directed at the servants, though sometimes Madam Dua and her two daughters were the target of her attacks. Only the male members of the family were spared. I quickly wrote off Madam Kassab as little more than a spoiled child.

Beyond members of the Kassab family, my world was reduced to the household staff, where the racial and ethnic hierarchy that defined our work roles carried over to our interactions with one another. Sri Lankan interacted with Sri Lankan and Filipino with Filipino, which left Almaz and me to spend all our time together. The two part-timers were also African women—one was from Eritrea and the other from Ethiopia. Almaz, who was good friends with both, called them "the twins" because of their physical similarities. We looked forward to their visits, which generally took place every other weekend or whenever extra help was needed. Taken together, the household was an eclectic mix of people, half of whom dedicated their lives to maintaining a sterile, tedious existence for the other half. "The whole world is right here in this house," observed Almaz one day. "Those who have things and those who do not. These are the only two groups in the world; everything else is meaningless."

As I became familiar with my job and the inner workings of the household, I worked on my "traditional" Himba clothing, usually at night when I was supposed to be off duty. Madam Dua supplied me with a faux-fur blanket with a leatherlike backing that was entirely inadequate for the task; each time I cut off a strip, the fur came undone from the leather, requiring hours of sewing and gluing each night. The old lady oversaw the entire project, carefully inspecting my work each week. I could not help but notice that it was similar to the costume Ming had made me wear in the DRC, particularly in terms of the general principle that less was more. It felt like I was making lingerie more than anything else, which supported my belief that there was a man behind Madam Dua's guiding hand.

9

My DAILY ROUTINE in the Kassab household continued virtually unchanged for the next couple of weeks. Each day, I awoke to clean the same things that I had cleaned the day before. The things I cleaned were already so clean that it was impossible to tell the difference. The only things that were not clean were those that some family member had touched. I could tell where each individual had been by the little messes they left scattered about the house. In reality, that is all I did—follow each member of the family around the house and clean up after them. It was amazing, I thought, that these people lived their lives knowing that every piece of food they dropped on the floor, every tissue they discarded, every object they moved or touched, and every smudge mark or blemish they left in their wake during the course of the day would be cleaned, removed, or restored to its original state of perfection by somebody else, usually within the hour. It was like tracking a herd of elephants by the piles of shit they left behind as they crossed an otherwise featureless desert plain, except I had to pick up each pile of shit as I went along, and I had to do it every day and for no real reason at all. I joked about this to Almaz one day, who laughed and said, "Maybe that is what your elephant dreams mean. They have led you here so that you can be an elephant tracker." But I did not think so.

Even so, I quickly became an expert on the movements of the Kassab family and their servants. Like elephants, everyone wandered the house and occupied its spaces in relation to how much power and authority they wielded. Dr. Kassab and his youngest son moved about like solitary bulls, roaming with total impunity and going wherever they pleased.

Their movements were the most random and hardest to predict, which sometimes made it difficult for the servants. Fortunately, the father and son were rarely home. The daily routines of Madam Kassab and her daughters were much more likely to revolve around the house. But they maintained their own internal pecking order that determined where and when they moved about. And even Madam Kassab—like an old cow—gave way when the bulls were around, either remaining in the kitchen when her husband was home or shadowing him in a deferential manner, ready to serve. The servants, of course, were silent apparitions, hovering or flittering about like shadows, tangible only when called upon.

I grew to despise Madam Dua with each passing day. Beyond the verbal abuse and the periodic slapping and kicking, the old lady held some unusual ideas about the health and well-being of the servants, ideas that might better be defined as a special form of torture. Most of her remedies were based on the application of heat to address injuries, aches and pains, or even something Madam Dua described as "temperature imbalances," which she associated with a lack of concentration or general apathy leading to poor work performance. Any servant suffering from the latter would be made to sit in the baking sun in the late afternoon, sometimes for an hour or more, which in Dubai was pushing the limits of what most humans could endure. Madam Dua prescribed this treatment in a seemingly random manner and regardless of whether the individual had actually complained of anything or not. Of course, everybody quickly learned not to complain. But the old lady was the ultimate authority on the matter, and the fact that everything hinged on work performance made it difficult to believe that her diagnoses had anything to do with health. I was subjected to the treatment several times within the first two weeks of my arrival. Each episode made my head throb until I thought it would burst, and one time I vomited. Fortunately, as I learned to do my job to the old lady's satisfaction, I seemed to build up my immunity to her so-called temperature imbalances and was no longer subjected to the treatment.

But of all Madam Dua's therapeutic measures, the one most feared among the servants involved something called *wasm*, which she claimed was an ancient form of medicine among the desert-dwelling Bedouin tribes of the region. She practiced wasm on any servant who experienced an injury or complained of sore muscles, achy joints, abdominal pains, or anything else that seemed localized or acute. Again, the servants learned not to complain and tried to hide their injuries or any outward signs of distress, but the old lady had a keen eye and was always on the lookout for abnormalities or physical irregularities. Sometimes she simply decided that a particular individual was in need of wasm.

The procedure was simple: Three or four small iron rods were heated in a coal burner until they glowed red-hot. As the rods were heating, Madam Dua had the patient lie down and expose the injured or aching area. Taking a marker pen, she carefully drew a series of symbols on the patient's skin. The symbols held a mysterious meaning only she knew, but it was clear that each was associated with a specific condition or part of the body. Symbols included a combination of dots, plus signs, *x*'s, circles, triangles, lines, and other things. The only thing servants could be certain of was that more symbols equaled more pain, since the markings essentially served as templates for the application of the iron rods. When they were sufficiently heated, Madam Dua pressed the rods against the person's skin, using the symbols as a guide, explaining how the procedure increased blood flow to the area and stimulated movement. Nobody knew what to make of the old lady's wasm treatment; the only thing it seemed to do was cause excruciating pain and extensive blistering. I noticed that Madam Dua seemed to take a bizarre pleasure from doling out the treatment; her weathered face twisted into a slanted grin and her eyes gleamed with delight as her patients screamed and writhed beneath her.

In addition to avoiding wasm and other forms of abuse from Madam Dua, I learned different ways to resist my captors. And that is how I always thought of them—as captors, not as employers or managers or sponsors. To me, the Kassab family was no different than the SPLA soldiers in South Sudan. As far as I was concerned, I was still a hostage. But now I was determined to do as little as possible to help those who had taken my freedom. I provided Madam Dua with few details about my personal life, despite the old lady's best efforts to find out more. I even began a misinformation campaign of sorts, telling her that I was actually an orphan and providing a long and totally fictitious account of how I was really from the Vambo tribe rather than the Himba, and that it only seemed like I was Himba because of traditional inheritance and adoption laws. I explained how my adopted Himba parents really did not care for me and thought of me as little more than a goat to be traded once I had reached a certain age. "That is why I am even here now," I explained, "because they never cared about me and were very happy to be rid of me." On occasion, I even managed to work up some tears, begging Madam Dua to adopt me so I could stay "as a special member of the family forever." I knew the entire notion was absurd, but I took great pleasure in seeing the look of confusion on the old lady's face. I also wanted to undermine any strategy to blackmail me by sending shameful photos to my parents. I kept my adoption story alive by alluding to it every now and then, mostly in an indirect manner so as not to overplay my hand.

I also performed as little work around the house as possible, an act of resistance made easier by the fact that the place was generally spotless anyway. I even worked out a series of sounds with Almaz—ranging from coughs and sneezes to banging our mops on the floor—to warn each other when a particular person was approaching. When nobody was around, we simply stopped working altogether. We also developed a method of stealing food from the kitchen that went completely undetected by Madam Dua and others. With the assistance of the Pakistani gardener, we accumulated a small stash of items that we hid behind some loose bricks in the gardener's shack. I felt a kind of strength in doing things like this; it made me feel like I was more than just a poor, suffering girl. With each act, I was placing a pebble on a pile that was becoming bigger and bigger. Eventually, pebbles would become rocks, rocks would become boulders, and the pile would become a mountain. This slow accumulation of effort and movement, this creation of something out of nothing, seemed to me to have a much stronger connection with my elephant dreams than anything else.

I knew that I was having an influence on Almaz too, so much so that my friend was beginning to reconsider her own situation. "Maybe we can open up a shop together in Addis Ababa," she told me one day. "We can have a boutique and sell clothes, and I can be together with my children again. You can start a new life in Ethiopia. It would be nice, yes? To be friends and business partners?" I smiled and agreed that it would be nice.

As we grew closer, Almaz confided in me and told me more about herself and how she had ended up in Dubai. As it turned out, her original story about being recruited by the Kassab family and placed directly in their home upon arrival was not exactly the truth. She said she was sorry for misleading me but confessed to being ashamed of what had actually happened. "We are friends now," she said, grasping my hands. "Friends are honest with each other."

Almaz admitted that she never had a husband who died in a car crash. In reality, she had never been married. While she did have two children to support in Ethiopia, they were from different men who never provided assistance and had long since been out of the picture. She had tried for some time to find a decent job in her own country but with no luck. Finally, her best friend had told her about a recruitment agency in Addis Ababa that was looking for women to work in a five-star hotel in Dubai. At the time, Almaz had never even heard of Dubai, but the job paid well and promised many benefits, and the photos of the hotel were the most beautiful she had ever seen. Of course, the driving force behind her decision was her children, and like every mother she wanted them to have the life that she could never have. So in the end it was an easy decision for her. Before she knew it, she had completed the orientation course, signed a contract, and was on a flight to Dubai with a dozen other women.

Things did, in fact, go badly for Almaz when she arrived at the airport in Dubai. As she had told me earlier, her group was immediately whisked away to a back room, where several men and a woman took their passports and identity documents. The woman strip-searched them and took everything they had—money, cell phones, anything important. Those who protested were immediately shouted down and threatened with jail. It was an overwhelming ordeal, especially for a group of women who had never been out of Ethiopia before and had just experienced their first plane trip. Like Almaz, every woman was in a desperate situation back home: struggling to support their children or other dependents, abandoned by their husbands or boyfriends, and virtually destitute. They huddled together against the back wall of the tiny room, stunned into silence by everything that was going on around them. When they were told to sign new contracts, written entirely in Arabic, they signed.

It was at this point that the truth of what happened to Almaz completely diverged from what she had told me before. Instead of being sent directly to the Kassab household or, for that matter, to a luxury five-star hotel, she was taken to a dingy nightclub and put to work as a "server," a meager euphemism in Dubai for a sex worker. Her manager was a rough, overbearing Iranian man who raped her repeatedly during the first couple of weeks. He told her it was a way to "break her in." But it was also a means of shaming her, because he knew that, as a defiled woman, Almaz would be left with few if any options beyond sex work, which made her less likely to run away or return home. In fact, and as Almaz quickly learned, "breaking in" the new women was a common practice, not only at that particular place but also at many of Dubai's most popular nightclubs. Despite her experience, Almaz did try to run away in the beginning, but she was immediately caught and thrown in jail. The police called her manager, who came down and severely beat her right there in the cell as two policemen stood by and watched.

As Almaz told her story, she described the realities of working in one of Dubai's most notorious nightclubs. Each night, an endless parade of drunk tourists and businessmen from around the world appraised her in the cold, fierce manner of men without burden or expectation. When they purchased her, they demanded the same things, did the same things, threw the same useless words at her day after day, night after night, until she learned to anticipate everything they said or did and respond automatically. Many had strange fantasies and desires, but Almaz would not go into detail about those, telling me only that she learned to anticipate and finesse those as well.

One of her most disturbing memories from that time involved men who requested very young girls. In most cases, the man specifically wanted the girl to be a virgin. The women referred to these men as "cherry poppers"; they made up a surprisingly large portion of the overall clientele, despite the fact that sex with a virgin was an extremely expensive service because the inventory had to be replenished constantly. If the man was drunk or less discerning, the manager simply offered him any girl and claimed she was a virgin. In fact, several girls, all of whom were seasoned veterans at acting afraid and uncertain, were kept on hand for just such occasions.

Almaz often wondered aloud at how, after a while, a person could become used to almost anything. "It became a job like any other job," she once told me. "I was making a lot of money, more than I could ever imagine making in my life. And I was able to send much of it back home to my children." She would have made even more, she explained, but the recruitment agency took its cut, which included a "finder's fee," for the cost of the plane ticket to Dubai and room and board at the nightclub. She was never quite certain of the remaining balance on her debt; she was told only that it would take years to pay off. Sometimes she wondered if her best friend back in Addis Ababa, the one who had told her about the job in the first place, had been paid for recruiting her, and how much she actually knew about the life she was sending Almaz to. "Such things can make you crazy with doubt," she once told me. I understood exactly what she meant.

Almaz also talked about the role of roving "agents" in Dubai's nightclub scene. These were individuals who worked on behalf of a particular client—maybe another nightclub or a wealthy individual—by actively "hunting" for women to come work for them. When agents passed through their club, Almaz told me, the women were made to line up in front of them so they could take photos to pass along to their clients. If their clients liked what they saw, they bought out the woman's debt, and her contract and all of her identity documents were transferred to them. Almaz told me how these lineups resembled auctions, where multiple agents bid on a particular girl, shouting over one another while taking directions from their clients over the phone. Sometimes agents took the girls in the back. "For a test drive," Almaz explained.

Almaz herself was selected by an agent about six months into her job at the nightclub. The agent worked for Dr. Kassab's eldest son—a man all the girls referred to as the Jackal—and just like that she was transferred to the Kassab household to work as a maid. Initially, she thought it strange that someone would hire a maid from a nightclub, but she quickly discovered that there were other job responsibilities. Whenever he was in Dubai, the Jackal hosted a series of parties, or what Almaz and all the women associated with these parties referred to as "special events." The guests, as Almaz described them, were all "big men"—businessmen, politicians, United Nations officials—men of power and influence. Many were white men from the United States and Europe. Special events were lavish, well-catered affairs that usually ran over the course of an entire weekend. Some were held in massive tents in the middle of the desert. The women were there to serve and pleasure the men in every possible manner. The Jackal liked to brag that his "harem" included women from around the world and that he personally selected each one for her exotic beauty and because she represented a particular country or region. In between special events, many of the women worked, like Almaz, as domestic servants in various households.

"It is not so bad," Almaz told me. "I do not make as much money as when I worked at the nightclub, but I do not have to fuck as much for a living. And the men are still the same. It makes no difference if they are rich and powerful; it is the same hungry look in their eyes." She shrugged her shoulders. "And so that is how it works here. And it is what you should expect now that the Jackal will be returning home. It is why you are here."

———

One evening, Almaz approached me and told me that we would be taking a break from our regular duties the following day. The eldest son—the Jackal—was returning from an extended business trip in several days, and we were to clean his apartment and prepare it for his return. I was glad for the break and eager to get a sense of Dubai and the general surroundings, especially since I had not once stepped off the property since arriving over a month earlier. My life had already become a dreary, lifeless existence, and I yearned to find out more about the world around me. Toward that end, I asked Almaz about the eldest son, but she offered few details. In fact, she seemed strangely quiet.

But I was determined to know more about the so-called Jackal and redoubled my efforts the next day. I had begun to realize that my ignorance was one of the greatest barriers to actually doing something about my situation. My lack of knowledge was more than just frustrating; it was deeply annoying. I had always seen myself as an intelligent and inquisitive learner and had taken a great deal of pride in figuring things out. I needed to become that person again. But everything that had happened to me combined with the daily routine of cleaning the Kassab house had put me in a mind-numbing trance. Endurance and resistance were important, but they were nothing without action. And action required knowledge. That was the next step.

Early the next day, a van arrived for Almaz, Madam Dua, and me. As we drove into the city center, we passed buildings that were increasingly tall and intimidating. The streets were neat and meticulously cared for. It was unlike anything I had ever seen before; it felt like we were winding our way through a narrow river gorge set between mountains of glass. Even the photos my uncle Gerson once showed me of Namibia's capital city—Windhoek—looked nothing like this. Everything here was glass and metal and hard surfaces with sharp angles, as if it had all been created just yesterday; it all seemed so modern and new. As I stared out the tinted window of the van, I realized that I had never really understood what a city was, and it made me wonder if I could ever comprehend its inhabitants and what they were capable of.

We arrived at a soaring building of twisted glass and burnished metal. Pulling around back, we exited the van and hurried to keep up with Madam Dua, who led us briskly past a security guard and through a maze of concrete hallways to a freight elevator. I had never ridden in an elevator before and felt a funny, bubble-like sensation in my head and stomach as we climbed forever upward. I prayed I would not get sick. Almaz must have noticed my queasiness—she smiled reassuringly.

The elevator doors opened to reveal a plush hallway lined with rich, deep carpets and brilliant chandeliers. There were mirrors everywhere. We followed Madam Dua silently down the hallway to a set of massive, elaborately carved doors. Producing a key from the folds of her robe, the old lady unlocked the doors to reveal a luxurious room of immense proportions. The general interior and furnishings seemed to mirror Dubai itself, consisting mostly of glass and bright metal objects that reminded me more of a perfume section at a department store or some kind of museum than someone's home. The far wall was lined with gigantic floor-to-ceiling windows that looked out onto the city. As with the Kassab house, I wondered how we were expected to clean a place that already looked so perfect and immaculate. Madam Dua stepped inside and Almaz followed, but I stood silently by the door, feeling a little overwhelmed as I tried to absorb everything that lay before me. I eyed the windows on the opposite side of the room uncertainly, conscious that I had only been above the second floor of any building once or twice in my entire life. I tried to remember if Opuwo had any buildings with more than two floors.

Madam Dua gave Almaz some last-minute instructions before leaving us for the day, informing us that she had to run errands and would return later that evening. "Do not leave this place," she warned us. "Do not go into the hallway. Do not let residents see you—not even your shadow. It disturbs them. Lock this door behind me." As she was leaving, she gestured toward me and said to Almaz, "You are in charge of this one. Make sure she knows her job." I closed and locked the door behind Madam Dua, glad to be rid of the old lady for a day.

As we prepared for work, Almaz noticed my reluctance to go near the windows. She laughed and said, "I was also afraid to approach these windows when I came here for the first time. We are very high, but it is safe. You can see all of Dubai and even the sea from here. We are like birds." She stood by the windows and motioned me over. "Come," she said. "You will not fall." Carefully, I made my way across the room to stand beside my friend. I laughed nervously and felt a small rush of excitement as I gazed out across the city to the water, which joined with the horizon in a whitewash of haze and wispy clouds.

"Where does this water go?" I asked Almaz.

"It goes everywhere," she replied. "It connects with everything all over the world. Big ships come and go from Dubai all the time."

"To Africa?" I asked.

"Oh yes. Even to my home, to Ethiopia." Almaz pulled me close and lowered her voice to a whisper. "We must work now," she said. "In this place, there are cameras everywhere watching us. So you must always show that you are working. Even if something looks clean, you must clean it anyway. Come and I will show you what we must do."

Almaz led the way to a small room off the kitchen filled with cleaning supplies. Sitting on a bench, she said, "There are no cameras in this room, so we can be free here, but we cannot remain long."

"This man is wealthy," I observed quietly.

Almaz nodded her head. "Oh yes. The Jackal is very wealthy." She paused and leaned back against the wall, looking very tired all of a sudden. "He is also a very bad man," she said, sighing. "I have been sparing you this because it is always much better when he is away on business. But I must tell you about the Jackal now. You see, he loves women. How should I say . . ." Almaz narrowed her eyes, fixing her gaze on the opposite wall as she searched for the right words. "As I told you before, he loves to . . . collect women . . . from all over the world. And show them to his friends during parties and . . . special events. Sometimes he buys and sells them . . . or just trades them . . . their visas and passports. If he likes you, then you remain." She added, "That dress . . . or costume . . . you have been making . . . it is for the Jackal. If he wants a woman from your tribe, he snaps his figures and makes it so. I am sure it is why you are here now. He wanted a . . . a . . ."

"Himba girl," I offered.

"Yes," Almaz said. "It is the same with me. He wanted me because I am from Ethiopia."

Over the past few weeks, I had put most of the pieces together already. Even so, it was good to finally confirm once and for all that this man—the Jackal—was the one responsible for my entire ordeal. It was he who had been on the other end of the line when Ming was describing me on the phone; it was he who had requested the photos and the video. I was the Jackal's "special order," and Dubai was the "special place." It was strange to think that after everything I had been through I was now standing in the apartment of a man who could simply stretch his arms across all of Africa and snatch up a young girl from the deserts of the Kunene. But it was him, I knew that for certain now.

"Are all the girls who work with us in this . . . position?" I asked.

"It is all different," Almaz said. "Some are just servants . . . just in their jobs. Some are here sometimes and making money in other ways at other times. Some are just making money at special events by sleeping with men. It is always different, always changing. Many come and go."

"And you?"

"Ah. I am a beautiful woman, like you. So we are together. For now. Until his tastes change. It is not in our hands."

I considered these words for a moment. "We must find a way to make it in our hands," I said.

Almaz eyed me curiously for a few moments. Finally, she shrugged her shoulders and smiled. "For now, we must work."

Over the next several days, I badgered Almaz for more information about Dubai and possible ways we could free ourselves from the grip of the Kassab family. I even approached Almaz's friends, the twins, and peppered them with the same questions. Although the twins worked for the Kassab household as part-time maids, they commuted in from one of the labor camps near the city center, where they shared a room with a group of other women. While they worked at the eldest son's special events, they also did sex work on the side. They explained that while the risk was greater, their "outside jobs" were also more lucrative because they were able to keep most of their earnings. They worked for the Jackal only because he was also their sponsor under the kafala system. I asked them if there was anybody in the labor camps who could possibly help me return home.

"You can run away and hide in the camps," one of the twins answered. "Many women do it. But then you are an illegal in the country, so you must be smuggled out somehow. There are many who will take you to Djibouti, but their services are very expensive. How will you make that money unless you sell your body? But you are beautiful; you will make a lot of money very quickly. And it is not so bad."

I emphasized that I did not want to sell my body. In fact, that was one of my main reasons for wanting to escape.

The first twin laughed in response. "Then you have a problem. I do not know a way," she said.

But the second twin interjected, "There is Dr. Mal. He will help you go anywhere in North or East Africa. But you must pay with your body."

I opened my mouth to protest again, but she cut me off. "No, not like that. Not sex. He will take your . . . what is it? What is the word? Here." She placed her hand on her abdomen, then, looking uncertain, slid it across to her back.

"Kidney," said the first twin.

"Yes, kidney. He will take your kidney. That is his price. And for that he will make a deal with you. He has helped runaways before. I know this because they have the big scar here." Again, she traced a line on her body, angling up from her waist and around her side toward her back. "Very ugly scar. Men will not like that . . . in case you wish to sell your body in the future."

Seeing the confused look on my face, the first twin said, "People here want strong kidneys. Their own kidneys are not so good. It is because they are fat and lazy. They have bad kidneys. They pay big money for a nice one. Dr. Mal will do the cutting for you. But it is dangerous business."

"But this way you are not selling your whole body," the second twin offered, giggling. "Just the parts."

―――――――――

I deliberated for some time over the twins' suggestion to sell a kidney. I asked Almaz why kidneys were so valuable. She told me that it had something to do with the high rate of diabetes among the Arabs in the country. She had heard that many Emirati traveled the world in search of kidneys. More recently, however, they had begun to tap into the country's large population of migrant workers, who were increasingly seen as a local solution to the problem. After all, she explained to me, it was easier and cheaper to bring the kidney to you rather than travel around the world in search of one. She had even heard that some people hired domestic servants with the intention of coercing them into donating their kidneys. Repeating what the twins had said, Almaz believed that kidneys were in high demand because the Arabs had ruined their own by being fat and lazy. "You see how we do all the work for them," she argued. "Now they do nothing but eat their pizzas and hamburgers, drive their cars everywhere, play their video games, and watch their TVs." She waved her arm dismissively. "Eh, they are just like Americans."

As far as the mysterious Dr. Mal and his clinic were concerned, Almaz was unable to dig up any details about the man or the procedure. She warned me that it would be risky; not only was the surgery illegal if performed by someone like Dr. Mal, who was not officially registered as a doctor in the UAE, but also even talking about it was considered taboo. More importantly, she stressed, were the health risks. There were whispers of girls dying shortly after the doctor performed the surgery.

But the more I turned it over in my head, the more plausible it became. How important could a kidney be? Even if a handful of girls died, many others lived and presumably gained their freedom. I decided that it was at least worth a visit to Dr. Mal's clinic. The twins agreed to arrange a meeting. However, they first had to find out the clinic's exact location, which turned out to be as much of a mystery as everything else.

Finally, the opportunity presented itself at the end of December, 2007. Madam Kassab, exhausted following an extended shopping trip to London and in the throes of what the staff referred to as one of her "long headaches," made the extremely rare decision to kick everyone out of the house for two days. With nowhere else to go, Almaz and I made plans to stay with the twins, who were able to track down Dr. Mal. They learned that his clinic changed locations on an almost continual basis, so it took a full day of furiously working their connections to find it. Finally, they traced its current location to an old tenement building in the densely populated Al Satwa district. We made plans to visit the next day.

The building was located on a narrow, busy street crammed with discount fabric shops and cheap restaurants. From the moment we entered the neighborhood, I felt a sense of foreboding. My anxiety grew as we explored the building itself, finding Mal's clinic only after passing through the greasy kitchen of a run-down Palestinian restaurant, navigating a narrow alleyway crisscrossed with drying laundry, and climbing a flight of dingy stairs to the third floor. Once there, we had to squeeze past several old men who sat on the landing smoking a hookah, which filled the stale air with an acrid, tarry odor.

After some additional exploring, we located a door with a crude, handwritten sign on it that read simply MAL. We stepped inside to find a large room skimpily furnished with a handful of plastic chairs and a folding table. Hanging on the wall above the table was a faded poster with the words UNDERSTANDING THE KIDNEY. There was a complicated illustration of what was presumably the kidney itself, including its approximate location in the human body. I noted that it was roughly where the twins had said it was, at least based on the scars they had seen on other women. Two girls who looked to be patients sat stoically in the plastic chairs while a third sat behind the folding table, lethargically thumbing away on her cell phone. An oddly familiar odor permeated the room, but I could not place it.

The girl behind the table glanced up as we approached. "Yes?" she said. "Can I help you?" And then almost as an afterthought, she added, "Welcome to the Mal Clinic."

Exchanging uneasy glances with Almaz, I responded, "We are here to ask about the operation"—I motioned toward the poster—"to remove the kidney."

The girl sat up a little straighter. "Yes, it is an unnecessary organ if you are healthy," she offered without prompting. "Dr. Mal will remove it for you—and even pay you a great deal of money to do it because it is needed by sick people." She launched into a long explanation about the kidney and why it was so prized, confirming Almaz's explanation that diabetes—type 2 diabetes, to be exact—was, in fact, the cause. She discussed the high rate of type 2 diabetes in the UAE and emphasized how an increasing number of people—children, in particular—suffered from the disease. With what almost seemed like a sense of pride, she raved that the UAE was among the top ten countries in the world with the highest rates of diabetes. "Many experts place us as high as number two!" she gushed, practically jumping out of her plastic chair. She repeated that many children suffered from the disease, though this time she contorted her face into an exaggerated expression of pity that prompted a loud snort from Almaz.

When she was finished with the first half of her pitch, the girl eyed me sharply. "How would you feel," she asked, "if you could pay off your debts and purchase a plane ticket home all on the same day?" Without bothering to wait for an answer, she asserted that offering up a kidney would allow me to do just that. "And go home with a pile of cash!" she beamed. She seemed to easily anticipate my situation, even mentioning that it would take years working as a domestic servant to make as much money as I could by selling my kidney.

Satisfied with her effort, the girl sat back and concluded with certainty, "So when can I schedule you for the operation? You can come and go on the same day. It is a very simple procedure. Can you come Tuesday?"

Throughout the girl's speech, I had felt a growing sense of unease. Before coming to the clinic, I was not sure what to expect—maybe a nurse or a doctor to explain things in a certain manner, like the way the doctor did when I broke my ankle as a little girl and had to visit the hospital in Opuwo. I remembered thinking at the time how the doctor spoke with the same authority and respect as a Himba headman. I liked that. But something was not right here. Dr. Mal was nowhere to be found; it was strange that he did not examine or even talk to potential patients prior to operating on them. Instead, he left everything to a silly girl in an empty room whose only job was to deliver a high-pressure sales pitch to anyone who walked in off the street. There was something unseemly about it. Not only that, I felt a creeping sense that something was being hidden from me. Almaz's warnings of all those girls who had died after a visit to the invisible Dr. Mal came flooding back.

Suddenly, I realized that the strange odor I had been struggling to identify was, in fact, blood. It had been difficult to distinguish at first, especially against the mix of pungent smells wafting up from the Palestinian restaurant on the bottom floor, as well as the clammy stench of hookah smoke that percolated into the room from the hallway. But now I was certain. I turned and stared at the two girls sitting behind me and realized that what I had thought were looks of quiet composure were actually expressions of anxiety bordering on outright fear. I felt a rush of nausea as I tried to tune in to the conversation between Almaz and the girl behind the desk. Their exchange had become heated as Almaz expressed shock at the idea that the price of a kidney was negotiable.

I grabbed Almaz's arm. "Let's get out of here," I whispered. Almaz, needing no further prompting, nodded her head in agreement. With a parting grunt aimed at the girl behind the table, she quickly ushered me out. When we left the building and turned into an alleyway, I ducked behind a dumpster and got sick. I started to apologize, but my friend cut me off. "No," she said, shaking her head. "You do not have to explain. There is an evil there. I do not know what it is exactly, but there is an evil." She took my hand and squeezed it. "As your friend, I will never bring you to such a place again. God as my witness, I will never do that."

10

WITHIN A WEEK of the Jackal's return, plans were being made for one of his special events. Madam Dua had me try on my costume, which was little more than a short skirt and a pair of leather boots. The boots had such high heels that it took quite a bit of practice to walk in them. The old lady smeared various concoctions on my skin to mimic the effect of otjize—the red ocher mixture that Himba women used—before settling on a blend of oil, red henna, and one or two other ingredients. As an added touch, she had me wear clip-in hair extensions and an assortment of gaudy jewelry. There was nothing about the final ensemble that in any way resembled traditional Himba dress, but as Almaz said, "It is about making men believe in the picture they have in their heads—and that is all about sex. They do not actually want to fuck a Himba girl straight from the village. They want to fuck the picture in their heads."

Madam Dua made an effort to teach me the finer points of walking and moving about in a "stimulating manner," but she ultimately delegated that task to Almaz, who also told me what to expect and how to act around white men. She thought it would be easy for me. "You are a very beautiful woman, and that is where their attention will be," Almaz said. "Mostly you smile and speak with your body and your touch—not your words."

She told me that when it came to special events, all I could do was hope to be chosen by a good man who wanted me for the entire weekend, rather than a succession of men. But she warned me that good men were rare: "You should expect every man to have strange demands and desires and to do things to you that he would not consider doing to his wife." She knew that I did not want to be any part of it, but she reasoned that it was all inevitable anyway, so I might as well be as prepared as possible. "They want your body, so you must learn how to speak with it," she said. "Then you can make it work for you as much as possible. You must use it to influence the man. It is better than having nothing at all."

But Almaz also believed it would be some time before I attended a special event. "The Jackal will want you for himself for some time," she told me. "The old lady is a fool. She knows he likes to taste his women first. It is what he usually does. And he will want you when he sees you, maybe for a long time. So you must be prepared." Almaz hesitated and bit her lip, as if she wanted to say more. But she simply shook her head and repeated, "You must be prepared."

One evening, without warning, Madam Dua grabbed me by the arm and demanded that I come with her at once. It happened so suddenly that nobody even saw us leave, including Almaz, who was working in another part of the house. To my surprise, the old lady led me outside to a waiting van and told me to get in. It was only the third time I had left the Kassab household since arriving in Dubai.

We drove to the Jackal's apartment once again, pulling around back to the alleyway as before. Without a word, Madam Dua led me through the winding corridors to the freight elevator and up to the apartment. This time, however, she rang the buzzer. An older man opened the door, nodding silently and stepping aside to let us in. Clearly, we were expected.

The man disappeared as I followed Madam Dua to the bathroom off the master bedroom. I was familiar with the room—I had cleaned it during my previous visit. Still, I was struck by how large it was, guessing that it was half the size of my uncle's entire house in Opuwo. Its surfaces gleamed as if they had never been touched before.

Madam Dua turned to me. "Undress," she commanded. "Get in the shower and scrub yourself well. Make certain you are completely clean." She opened a cabinet under the sink and took out two bottles. "When you are finished, you must rub this oil all over your body. Everywhere." She pointed to the second bottle. "Then I will spray you with this." She turned on the shower. "Be quick but thorough. I will return in fifteen minutes."

Anxious as I was, I could not help but enjoy the shower. The water to the servants' quarters at the Kassab household had been turned off for the past week so workers could upgrade the sprinkler system. Like all the servants, I had been taking sponge baths from a plastic tub. So now, I tried to prolong every second of my shower while trying to put any thoughts of what might be coming next out of my mind.

I was still drying myself when Madam Dua returned. She looked put out and had me stand naked before her so she could apply the oil herself. She worked furiously, her bony hands scraping against my skin without care or hesitation. She then took the second bottle, which turned out to be a scented body spray, and sprayed me from head to toe. When she was finished, the old lady produced a pair of red stilettos and thong panties. "Now put these on," she commanded.

She led me into the master bedroom and stood me at the foot of the bed. It was a massive king-sized bed with an elaborately carved headboard and a beautiful, cream-colored comforter. "Now wait," the old lady said before leaving the room.

I must have waited an hour, maybe two. I watched the sun set slowly over the city; it left behind a brownish-red band on the horizon that dissolved into the night. I tried to prepare myself but did not want to think about who or what was coming for me. Focusing on my dreams, I pictured a large herd of elephants lumbering across the Kunene, moving nowhere and with purpose at the same time. It comforted me to think of their soft footfalls.

The man who eventually entered the room was in direct contrast to any image I had in my head. He was short, with slight, reedy features, and moved in an odd, abrupt manner, as if he were in a rush to be somewhere else. He crossed the room and peered at me with large, dark eyes. His front teeth were too large for his mouth and jutted out slightly under his thick black mustache.

Despite his small stature and odd appearance, he carried himself with an air of confidence—or perhaps just arrogance—as if he owned everything before him. He probably did, I thought, since I remembered him now from a family photo at the Kassab house and realized that this could only be the Jackal. Balancing a drink on his lap, he sat on the edge of the bed and continued to stare at me in a piercing and completely uninhibited manner.

"Walk back and forth," he said, in a voice that was surprisingly high. I walked to the bathroom door and back again, essentially naked before this strange man—my new owner. Sitting back on his elbows on the bed, he sipped his drink and continued to issue commands, making me pose in different positions. I did everything in silence; he never asked me a question or expected me to speak. I knew he was making himself hungry. I could see it in his eyes.

He ordered me to walk toward the window. I was almost there, trying not to look down because the height still frightened me, when I glimpsed his reflection in the window approaching me from behind. I closed my eyes just before he was on me.

I can only say that what the Jackal did to me that night—and all subsequent nights that I was called to his place—was on a whole different level; it was an entirely new kind of pain and humiliation that I had not yet known existed. It made me realize that the rapes I had experienced or witnessed up to that point were all done by amateurs—simple, foolish men who could not control themselves. Like baboons, their urges simply overpowered them and they did things without thinking. But the Jackal was a professional. He loved to be a giver of shame and pain; there was a grotesque pleasure in it for him. While I had met many rapists and abusive men by this point, I never knew one who enjoyed going about it in the slow, methodical manner of the Jackal. It was like he learned to control his urges by channeling them into prolonged stories of misery and degradation. I do not know how or where a human learns these stories. It is not important. The details are meaningless. I just know the Jackal was the sickest and cruelest of them all. As for myself, I learned thresholds of pain that I did not know I had. I learned what I could endure because I had no choice.

———————

Over the next six months, my routine became one of endless work punctuated by sudden, violent episodes of abuse at the hands of the Jackal. Each time I was summoned to his place, I prepared myself for a night of unspeakable cruelty, until each revolting act, each sexual deviance, became part of the routine, something to be endured to make it through the night. In that sense, the next morning was always a good thing because it represented the beginning of a period when I was not being abused. I tried to imagine myself as being on a long trek through the desert, having to endure brief yet intense intervals under the sun in order to reach the next village or water hole or shade tree, the next place of relative safety. The trick was to train myself to endure the heat by knowing that at some point it would not be there, even if just for a moment or a night or a few weeks—there would be a period of relative comfort. "Just keep walking," I would say to myself during those nights with the Jackal. "The shade tree is there in the distance. Just keep walking." *Elephant steps*, I thought.

And eventually I would reach it. After he was finished with me for the night, the Jackal sent me home—usually around 3:00 or 4:00 AM—at which point I was expected, as always, to work another sixteen-hour shift. The day after an episode with the Jackal was always difficult; my body was so racked with pain that I spent much of my time trying to hide from Madam Dua and members of the Kassab family so I could be sick and take short naps. I became adept at sleeping for a few minutes at a time, even if it meant leaning against the wall as I scrubbed the floor. I marveled at the human body's capabilities, how it could keep moving as the person inside slept.

There were several special events during this time, but I did not attend them. Almaz approached me after I had experienced a particularly bad night with the Jackal. "I should have prepared you better," she told me, shaking her head with a look of shame and pity. "It is like I said before, the Jackal likes to taste his women before he makes them available. It is normal. And what he does . . . how he enjoys hurting . . . it is normal too." She advised me to accept my circumstances and try to be strong. She told me that things would get better once the Jackal tired of me and moved on to the next woman. "It is his usual practice," she said. "Eventually, soon maybe, he will throw you away and make you available as just another girl for his special events. You will be with more men—powerful men—and they will treat you much better than the Jackal. It will be easier for you then." Since special events were made up of close business associates of the Kassab family, she warned me to be careful and submit to everything they wanted. "You do not want to get a bad review," she said. "It would make the Jackal angry, and you do not want to make that one angry."

No, I thought, *I do not want to make him angry.* Though I had never seen him angry, the Jackal still left me with a battered, aching body. I could only wonder what such a man was capable of when truly angry.

Eventually, things turned out as Almaz predicted. The Jackal called on me less frequently until the day came when I learned that I was to be included in the next special event. I felt relief more than anything else, hoping that it represented the end of my personal sessions with the Jackal. Yes, other men would rape me now, but perhaps they would be nicer to me. *Nice rapists*, I thought, and almost laughed.

On the morning prior to the special event, I climbed into a van full of women. In addition to Madam Dua, Almaz, and the twins, several white women were part of our group. I asked Almaz who they were.

"They are from Europe," she replied. "I think they are Russian. They are regulars at all of these events. You know some men prefer white women. And the Jackal likes to have a selection of women from around the world. These events are . . . known to be like this. That is why so many men wish to attend. But the Jackal only includes men who help him with his business interests. These events are special. They are . . . what is the word?"

"Exclusive," I offered.

"Yes," Almaz confirmed. "They are exclusive events."

Appraising my fellow passengers again, I said, "These are all very beautiful women."

"Oh yes," Almaz agreed. "That is what makes it exclusive." She motioned toward the white women. "They are professionals. Sex is their business."

"Prostitutes?" I asked.

"Yes," Almaz said. "But high-end prostitutes. They do not work on the streets like other girls. And they are very expensive. They only work events such as these and only serve very rich men."

This time we drove in the opposite direction of the city center, passing residential neighborhoods and small shopping centers until the buildings tapered off and vanished altogether, leaving behind a vast desert landscape. The air inside the van became thick and heavy. As I stared out the window at the endless sea of sand, I realized just how isolated I was in Dubai. Even if I attempted to run away, I thought, it would be difficult to get anywhere. I understood the harsh realities of the desert and knew that traveling by foot depended on an intimate knowledge of the land. And the environment that passed before me now was the most unforgiving one I had ever seen.

We drove for several hours before turning off the paved road and onto a dirt track that wound its way between enormous sand dunes, the largest of which threatened to overrun the road completely. Eventually, we crested a small rise and came upon a lush oasis of tall grass and palm trees. The contrast was so sudden and dramatic that it prompted small gasps of astonishment from the van's occupants. Speckled among the trees and tall grass was an array of large white tents with conical roofs that gave the place a festive, almost dreamlike appearance. At the far end, an enormous tent with two square cupolas dwarfed everything else, towering above the trees and commanding the entire scene.

As we exited the van and followed a narrow trail to the nearest tent, I caught a glimpse of an emerald-green pond at the center of the oasis. It was all so beautiful that I almost forgot why we were there.

Inside the tent, a dozen women were already busy putting on makeup, fixing their hair, or mending costumes. It was obviously a preparation area for the night's entertainment, or at least one facet of it. I could not get over how beautiful the women were. "These women are mostly from Iran," Almaz said. "They are in high demand by the white men. They all want to taste a Persian queen while they are here." She motioned to several girls sitting together at one table. "Look at these ones. They are very young girls, maybe thirteen or fourteen years old. But see? They are already professionals." The girls were chatting happily as they fixed their hair and applied their makeup, seemingly unfazed by their surroundings. One girl glanced sideways at me and snickered.

We found an empty table and sifted through a massive array of cosmetic items. There must have been enough for hundreds of women, I thought, though there were only about twenty-five in the tent.

When it came time to don our costumes, Almaz gestured to the other women and said, "You see? They are dressed like they come from all over the world. As I said, that is a big part of these events. The Jackal wants to display to his associates his selection of exotic and beautiful women." She repeated how his special events were well known among a certain discerning crowd.

I asked Almaz where the men came from. "They are from all over the world too," she answered. "Some are from here, but most, as you will see, are white men. Many are working for the United Nations here in Dubai or visiting from other bases around the world. They are very powerful men. Like I said before, they work on human rights during the day and fuck young girls behind their wives' backs at night."

As she fixed her hair, Almaz explained how a growing number of men who visited Dubai's brothel scene were from the United Nations or organizations associated with the humanitarian and international aid sector. She said it was a direct result of the government's efforts to transform Dubai into one of the largest humanitarian centers in the world. Toward that end, and in true Dubai fashion, an entire section of the city—the International Humanitarian City—was constructed from scratch. Since then, humanitarian and international aid workers had been pouring into the city and, quickly following their arrival, patronizing its infamous sex industry. Brothels and nightclubs directly catered to them; one famous brothel even described itself as the "United Nations of Prostitution." Escort services targeted these individuals by marketing their women as "sophisticated" or "worldly" and as being able to satisfy the demanding needs of global professionals. It was common for humanitarian organizations to provide their clients with girls in order to get contracts signed, close deals, and conclude lucrative business transactions. The international aid sector supplied such a huge number of clients, Almaz claimed, that there was even a term for them: "humanitarian johns."

"Yes, these humanitarians"—Almaz practically spit out the word as she inspected herself in the mirror. "We are all having angels and demons inside of us," she said under her breath.

As the women dressed, I could see that their costumes were meant to represent different parts of the world. Each costume was so scant, however, that there was hardly anything to work with; some were little more than strategically placed bits of cloth in the national colors of some mysterious foreign country. Almaz's costume consisted of an extremely short and very revealing white skirt—if it could be called that—with a matching top that was not much wider than a belt, which she tied somewhat futilely around her ample breasts. She caught me staring at her and shrugged. "It is not the traditional dress of my people; it is only a . . . suggestion of one." Staring at my own costume, she said, "Yours, of course, is the same—a suggestion."

I looked down at myself. Like the other costumes, mine was basically nonexistent and intended to be as revealing as possible. My breasts were completely exposed. With Almaz's help, I covered my body with the red mixture that was meant to simulate otjize. Madam Dua popped in and out of the tent all afternoon and seemed pleased with the results. She nodded assent before moving on to upbraid a girl who was struggling with her hair extensions.

"You are truly beautiful," Almaz said unexpectedly.

I was not sure how to respond; the comment seemed misplaced, given the context. Finally, I said, "I am dressed like a prostitute. Where I come from, prostitutes are not considered beautiful."

Almaz smiled encouragingly. "Hopefully, a nice man will choose you for the whole weekend. That is the best thing that can happen."

Madam Dua, who had stepped out of the tent for several minutes, suddenly rushed back in and clapped her hands in a flurry. "Girls who are in the first group, come with me now!" she shouted. Earlier in the day, we had been designated as belonging to one of two groups. The first group included seasoned veterans who had participated in one of the Jackal's special events before, while the second group, which was much smaller and included myself, consisted of girls with little to no experience.

Since she was part of the first group, Almaz gave me some final words of advice. "The men will be drunk by the time you come to the tent. That will make things go easier. You only need to walk around and greet them and laugh and smile at everything they say. I know many men will want you, but I will try to find a nice one for you. I will guide you to him when you come. Hopefully, the Jackal will not want you for himself. But he has just had you so I think he will want another girl. Look for me when you come. Remember: laugh and smile at everything." She made an exaggerated, toothy smile to emphasize her point, reminding me of how the white tourists smiled back in Opuwo.

After the first group left, I assessed the other "new girls." They were all very young, even younger than myself. "Where do you come from?" I asked a tall, slim girl with brown skin and large green eyes that had an almost haunted appearance.

"Morocco," she said.

"How did you come to be here?"

Shrugging her shoulders, the girl cast her eyes about nervously. "We needed the money, like everybody else."

I asked her if she was here by choice or had been forced, maybe even taken without warning and thrown into the back of a truck like myself. But the question only seemed to make the girl more nervous. "I cannot answer those types of questions," she finally said, before repeating, "We needed the money."

I listened as music filled the evening air and the raucous laughter and excited voices of the men grew louder. When the sun dipped behind the dunes and it almost seemed like we had been forgotten, Madam Dua finally returned, clapped her hands sharply once again, and ordered the second group of girls to follow her.

The path to the main tent was lit by torches, which in the half light cast flittering shadows on the surrounding dunes. The flames accentuated the carnivalesque atmosphere and created an eerie energy that was almost palpable. We sauntered through the tall grass in single file behind Madam Dua, trying to keep up with her brisk, determined pace. Bringing up the rear, I hesitated and gazed up at the evening sky. There were a dizzying number of stars. I said a silent prayer and tried to compose myself for the evening ahead.

The main tent was a tempest of activity. On a raised platform in the center, a live band bounced about as they played the animated, almost frantic music that I often heard coming from the radio in Madam Kassab's bedroom. Alongside the band, three scantily clad belly dancers weaved and undulated suggestively, pointing and beckoning around the room as if inviting different spectators to come join them on stage, though no one seemed to be paying much attention. The lone exception was a drunken, middle-aged white man who lingered nearby and swayed back and forth. He leered idiotically at the women as he spilled his drink down his shirtfront. In all, about twenty men were scattered about the tent, most reclining on pillows strewn about the heavily carpeted floor. A gaggle of boys who doubled as both waiters and busboys dashed between large, low-set tables packed with an assortment of food and drinks, diligently taking orders and removing dishes. The girls were mixed in with the men, lying alongside or in some cases on top of them, laughing and smiling at nothing in particular. They helped themselves to the food and drink as well. I searched for Almaz, but it was relatively dark inside the tent and clouds of cigar smoke swirled about. There was also an open firepit in the corner, where cooks were busy roasting a large piece of meat on a spit. And though the tent flaps immediately surrounding the pit were rolled up, thick plumes of smoke continued to waft inside. The entire scene was a whirlwind of noise and movement, as if the tent itself were about to burst from the excess and overindulgence that impregnated it.

As new arrivals, we were ushered onto the stage, where a short man dressed in a powder-blue sequined suit introduced us to the assembled crowd. Each girl was given an armband that had a large number printed on it, which the man referenced as he read from a card describing her pertinent details. When my turn came, he said, "Number twenty-five is a beautiful young princess from the primitive Himba tribe in southwest Africa. The Himba are known for their exotic beauty and sexual drive. And yes, she is a true African princess. She is a little shy, but you should not let that fool you. She will fill your night with wild memories straight from Africa!" Men hooted and whistled as I walked off the stage, where Madam Dua grasped me by the arm and thrust me toward the nearest table. "Go," she hissed. "Make certain you find a man tonight. I do not want to see you alone at any time."

I took several tentative steps toward the table but then was grabbed from behind. I turned to find Almaz's smiling face. "Come with me," she said, then laughed in an exaggerated manner, as if we were two schoolgirls having the time of our lives. While walking arm in arm with my friend across the tent, I locked eyes with the Jackal, who was chatting with two other men at a bar in the corner. For the first time since I had known him, he wore the white, ankle-length robe favored by Emirati men. He stood out sharply against the crowd of half-naked girls and white men dressed in tan slacks and checkered shirts. He peered at me for a brief moment before his attention was drawn away, as if I were somebody he recognized but could not quite place.

Almaz led me outside, where two white men were sitting by a fire, drinking and laughing. She whispered in my ear, "This man seems nice. I have not seen him before. Attach yourself to him." Releasing me, she crouched behind the second man—an older, heavyset man with thinning gray hair and a full beard who was busy gnawing on the stub of his cigar. She wrapped her arms around him familiarly, as if she had known him for many years, and glanced at the second man. She nodded toward me. "This is my friend. She is beautiful, yes?"

The man glanced up at me. He was younger than the other man, perhaps in his late forties, with a friendly, expressive face. He winked and smiled. His eyes moved down my body before quickly snapping back to my face, betraying a polite man with powerful, hidden urges. I had seen that look many times before, though on most men I had become familiar with since my abduction, those urges overwhelmed the politeness in an instant. This particular man reminded me of the white, middle-aged tourists I knew from Opuwo: pale skin, large, soft limbs, slightly bulging stomach, and an open face with an ever-present smile and attentive eyes. I noticed how well groomed he was; he was clean-shaven with neatly trimmed hair and nails that looked professionally manicured.

"Hello, my dear," he said with a pronounced twang. "Come and have a drink with us." He patted the cushion on the bench beside him. "I'm Mike," he said as I sat down beside him. He poured me a full glass of wine and proceeded to ask me a string of funny questions, again reminding me of the tourists back in Opuwo. But his easygoing manner—combined with the wine—relaxed me, and I allowed myself to answer his questions, though I was careful not to reveal too much about myself.

Mike was an American who was in Dubai working for the United Nations. He mentioned that most of the other partygoers worked for the United Nations as well, though for different agencies. He was unusually talkative, either because he was drunk or just a naturally open person, and offered up a surprising number of details about himself. At the same time, he asked many probing questions about my own background, including where I was from and how I had come to Dubai. It never crossed his mind that I might be here against my will. As we continued to chat, I felt a nagging sense of frustration with the man; his questions and comments were extraordinarily naive, especially for a person with such obvious education and experience. I wondered how someone who was so curious and asked so many questions could be so ignorant. But as the night wore on, I realized that Mike the American was talking right through me. To him, I did not really exist at all.

Eventually, we returned together to his tent, the interior of which was almost entirely taken up by a large bed. He immediately took his clothes off and began clutching and grabbing at me, initially in a boozy stupor, but as he became aroused he seemed to snap out of it. The friendly demeanor he had maintained all evening vanished in seconds as he forced himself upon me. He recorded everything with his cell phone, even setting up a small tripod to hold it. When he brought out a box filled with his "sex tools," as he referred to them, he really got down to business. When I saw Almaz again, I thought, I would rebuke her for making me believe there could possibly be a "nice one" among such men. With that thought in mind, I set my jaw and endured the night as well as I could.

Following breakfast the next morning, most men attended one excursion or another. A large group drove straight into the desert on quad bikes, while the Jackal took a second, smaller group somewhere nearby to give them a demonstration of falconry, a particular passion of his. When everyone departed, an eerie silence descended on the camp. Of the handful of men who stayed behind, most remained in their tents in the company of one or more of the girls. Before leaving with the group of quad bikers, Mike the American told me he would look for me upon his return.

"If he wants you a second night, then you cannot deny him," Almaz told me after I recounted the night's events. "I am sorry that I introduced you to him, but the truth is that most of these men have . . . evil spirits to feed." Beyond these meager words, Almaz offered surprisingly little comfort or compassion, even lightly chastising me for being so naive at this point.

When the American returned later that evening, he sought me out as promised, and I was forced to remain by his side throughout the night. By the time we went back to his tent, he was noticeably drunker than the previous night. He continued to drink in the tent as he set up his phone to record the night's coming activities. Stripping off his clothes, he lay on the bed and mumbled something that sounded to me like a command to lie on top of him. By that point, however, I though he might be on the verge of passing out, so I remained where I was and watched him closely. Within minutes, he had passed out and was snoring loudly. A sense of relief washed over me. I knew we were leaving early the next morning, so I would be far away before he ever woke up. Turning to leave, my eyes landed on the man's wallet, which he had placed next to the phone on its little tripod. I glanced back at his prone figure and, without really knowing what I was looking for, grabbed the wallet and began rifling through it. I discovered photos of the man with what I could only assume were his wife and children, an American driver's license from the state of Virginia, and more bank cards than I had ever seen. I also found a business card with all of his contact information, including phone numbers and addresses in Dubai and the United States. It stated that he worked for the United Nations World Food Programme. Judging by his impressive title and credentials, he was a very big boss of some kind.

I took the business card, knowing he would never miss it, and placed the wallet back on the table. But then I realized with a shock that the phone had been recording me the entire time. *I have to delete the video,* I thought. Unscrewing the phone from its tripod, I fumbled around with it clumsily, trying to figure out exactly how it worked. But I had only ever used a cheap analog cell phone and had no experience with the more expensive touch-screen phones like this one. I pressed various buttons in a vain attempt to navigate through the different pages, but my efforts only seemed to make matters worse. Eventually, a mysterious warning sign popped up that left me completely uncertain of what to do next.

Rather than panic, however, a strange calm settled over me. I realized that I had nothing to lose. How much more could they humiliate me and treat me like an animal? What more could they do to me?

As I stood there in the American man's tent, staring blankly at the warning sign on his phone, I wondered how many violent rapes I had endured since being abducted almost a year and a half ago. Just at the hands of the Jackal alone, I could not possibly estimate the number of times I had been defiled. And now that he was through with me, he had tossed me aside to be the plaything of these bloated white men with their fake smiles and sunburned faces, these men with hidden lives and false morals. *No,* I thought, *I will not lie back and take this anymore.* "I must act," I whispered to myself. "I must act now." I said a little prayer and slipped from the tent, still clutching the cell phone.

11

I RETURNED TO MY WORK ROUTINE the following week, but hardly a minute went by when I did not think about the stolen phone, worried that Madam Dua or even the Jackal himself would confront me and demand to know where it was. I could not imagine the repercussions, certain only that they would involve a combination of physical violence and sexual abuse. Each time I heard Madam Dua's quick, purposeful footsteps approaching, my heart skipped a beat.

I hid the phone in the garden shack where we had been stashing our stolen food. When I told Almaz, she became silent, staring at me in disbelief before asking, "What have you done?" I had not expected this type of reaction from her, and it only made the potential consequences of my actions all the more real.

While examining the phone later that night, we discovered that the battery was dead, and we did not have the right kind of cable to recharge it. I was almost relieved; I did not particularly want my friend to see the photos and videos that the American had taken. But Almaz sensed my worry and waved her hand dismissively, saying, "All these men like to take videos, you know. We are all forced to do similar things." She turned her attention to the phone and studied it more closely. "This is American," she said. "But it is available here in Dubai. The cable is easy to get. I will ask my friends to bring one when they next come." She returned the phone to its hiding place and asked to see the man's business card. She inspected it for a long time before letting out a heavy sigh, saying, "He is very high up in the United Nations. This does not surprise me. These special events are not for tourists—only the very powerful—only for men who can help the Jackal in some manner." She handed the card back to me. "And these men—you know they keep their lives on their phones. It is only a matter of time before he comes looking for it."

"What can I do?" I asked. And then I added with a note of defiance, "I am glad I took it."

Almaz eyed me curiously, as if seeing something she had never noticed before.

"We need to get this phone working," I said, feeling emboldened now. "So we can contact this man directly. We will make him listen to us."

———————

Several days later, I entered my tiny room to find Madam Dua searching through my things. "Something is missing," said the old lady without a trace of guilt or self-consciousness at being caught rifling through my personal belongings. "I must find it. Have you taken anything recently that does not belong to you? Do not lie to me, girl."

"I have not taken anything," I replied, determined not to cave in or back down at this point.

Madam Dua grunted and flung a box of tissues on the floor. There were few places to conceal anything in the sparsely furnished room. For once, the old lady looked tired, even a little defeated. "Stupid Americans," she mumbled more to herself than to me. "They are not responsible people." An awkward silence passed as the old lady, sitting in a plastic chair, clasped her hands and seemed to lose herself in contemplation.

She looked up at me suddenly, her deep-set eyes boring through me with a look of intense hatred. "You are lying. I will tell Master Kassab that you are lying and that you are hiding something. He wants to see you again, and I will bring you before him in a few days." She stood up, slapped me hard across the face, and exited the room.

I placed my hand on my face and worked my jaw, waiting for the pain to subside. I sensed something terrible was coming.

———————

The next day, I approached Almaz and begged her to contact the twins so they could bring the phone cord as soon as possible. Fortunately, Madam Kassab was throwing a dinner party the following day, so the part-time staff would be needed, and the twins were due to arrive early the next morning. Almaz borrowed a phone from a delivery boy who happened to be at the house and called her friends, who promised to bring the cord.

By the following night, I was navigating through the phone as I lay in bed. Fortunately, I had watched the American enter his four-digit passcode several times during our first night together. If it were not such a simple sequence of numbers, I never would have remembered it. Looking back on everything now, however, I realized that knowing his passcode probably factored into my decision to take the phone in the first place.

Now, with more time to search through the phone, it was easy to collect information on Mike the American. I discovered that he was married and had at least two children, one being my age. He was the oldest of several siblings, had parents with health problems, liked to golf, and lived in Virginia. He also had a second home in a place called Arizona. I even learned the name of his dog.

For the most part, he communicated with his wife through his phone's messaging app, which allowed me to sift through their conversations with ease. I learned that his wife and children remained in the United States while he divided his time between the States and Dubai, something they had been doing for over five years now. They had ironed out any problems related to trying to maintain a long-distance relationship, developing a yearly routine that seemed to work well for both of them. I was shocked at how much love and respect the man displayed for his wife; he anticipated her needs and responded with attentive care to everything she said. Their text messages made frequent references to phone conversations they had with each other, which occurred every few days. They talked a lot about their children—their hobbies, their soccer games, how they were doing in school, what they did with their friends, the parties they attended, the funny things they said and did—everything. They referenced the great time the family had during a recent vacation to the Caribbean. There were few indications of any serious problems or challenges. Mike the American had a nice family life. He and his wife seemed very happy. Everything was good.

His blessed life seemed to extend to his job as well. As I read his work e-mails, it was clear that he was very high up in the United Nations. He had a tremendous amount of authority; most e-mails involved delegating various tasks to a slew of subordinates. He communicated with high-level government officials from around the region—not just the UAE. There were discussions about refugees and the logistics involved with delivering food and humanitarian assistance to various locations around the world.

The more I looked through the phone, the more I thought about something my grandfather once told me: "A man with a big belly will only give away his fat when he is afraid for his life." I considered these words as I made myself watch the video of everything Mike the American had done to me that night.

———

It took one incident for everything to unravel. I was in the garden shack emptying garbage bins when Almaz came in carrying the broken shards of a vase. I recognized the pieces immediately; it was a particularly prized piece from Madam Kassab's extensive collection of vases, which were on display throughout the house. The side of Almaz's face was red, and a trickle of blood flowed from her lip and onto her chin. Drops of blood spattered the front of her work apron.

I rushed to my friend. "What has happened?" I asked. "Are you all right?"

Almaz brushed past me, tossed the broken shards into the trash bin, and launched into a long diatribe in Amharic, stopping only after she had reduced herself to tears.

Suddenly, Madam Dua rushed in. She snatched a small wooden stake from the gardener's workbench and began beating Almaz on the back of the head with it. Almaz screamed and doubled over, desperately trying to shield herself. But the old lady was in a mad fury and continued to rain down blows with astonishing speed and force. Almaz slumped against the back wall, leaning directly against the bricks where we hid our secret stash of food. I watched in shock as the bricks toppled in, revealing the large stash of items we had pilfered from the kitchen. Even more terrifying, the stolen phone sat in plain sight.

Madam Dua paused in midswing, her arm raised menacingly above her head. She hissed, "What is this?" Her head swung back and forth between the phone and me. She repeated herself, this time punctuating each word with a single, vicious swing of the stake. "WHAT—IS—THIS?" The blows came down hard against the back of Almaz's head and hands as she made feeble attempts to shield herself.

And then the old lady wheeled around and directly confronted me. Her thin lips were twisted into an angry snarl and her eyes were wide and set, as if she were under some kind of spell, conscious only of the need to inflict pain. Her whole body shook as she raised the stake high above her head and brought it down.

But I was ready for it. I stepped under the blow and drove my shoulder as hard as I could into Madam Dua's chest. As she fell backward, the old lady tripped over Almaz's crumpled body and, with a dull, sickening thud, struck the back of her head on the corner of the gardener's workbench. She landed in an awkward position beside Almaz, moaning and moving her head slightly. She appeared seriously hurt.

I helped Almaz back to her feet. My friend stood over Madam Dua's prone body for several seconds, staring down at her. Finally, she spat on the old lady and viciously kicked her in the side. She turned toward me and we simply stared at each other, trying to digest everything that had just happened in the span of a few minutes.

"We must go," Almaz said at last. I nodded and began to follow my friend out the door.

"Wait!" I exclaimed, suddenly remembering the phone. "We will need this." Almaz also snatched the keys to the front gate, which Madam Dua always kept on a small chain around her neck.

We set out through neighborhoods similar to our own, passing houses that were set well back from the street and concealed behind high walls and security fences. In most cases, the only thing visible above the wall was a thick nest of satellite dishes, antennae, and surveillance cameras. We felt painfully conspicuous against the indistinguishable landscape of neat, orderly streets and generic facades. I found a plastic bag and used it to wipe away the blood on Almaz's head and hands. I thought my friend looked unsteady on her feet. Even I felt a little light-headed in the midday sun.

Almaz believed our best chance was to hide in one of the migrant labor camps on the edge of the city. There, we would be anonymous, just two among thousands of runaways and invisible absconders with no real identity or documentation. We could then seek help from the twins, who would also keep us apprised of what was happening at the Kassab household. With that vague plan in mind, we set out toward the city center, where we would try to hitch a ride on one of the many buses that shuttled workers to and from the camps.

We tried to stay off the main streets and avoid the suspicious stares of people. But two unveiled black women walking around such neighborhoods in the middle of the day was an unusual sight. Every car that drove past slowed down so its occupants could gawk at us. On three different occasions, a car pulled up and a man leaned out the window to proposition us. One man in particular would not give up; he followed us for several blocks in his black BMW, whistling and calling after us from inside his car. He clearly assumed we were prostitutes.

We spotted the first police car as we scrambled through an alleyway and it sped past the entrance just ahead of us. We continued to stick to the back alleys as much as possible, dashing across streets and open spaces as quickly as we could. But after a while, we realized that the police were searching for us, patrol cars crossing back and forth as if in a coordinated search pattern. The empty, sterile surroundings of Dubai's wealthier neighborhoods made it difficult to hide or blend in, and we knew it was a matter of time before they discovered us. I cursed the blinding sun, which seemed to bear down on us like a spotlight.

Almaz seemed to be thinking the same thing. "Ech," she exclaimed, shielding her eyes and pressing her back against the wall in a vain attempt to retreat into the shade. "We need to get out of these neighborhoods," she muttered as the sweat trickled down the side of her face. "We are too obvious here. Everyone will see us."

I was just about to suggest that we climb over a wall and take our chances hiding in someone's yard when a car turned swiftly into the alley and roared toward us. We froze. There was nowhere to run. It was over.

But it was not the police. And it was not over. It was the man in the black BMW who had called out to us earlier. He rolled down a tinted window and said, "You two beauties can either come with me or you can go with the police. So which one will it be?"

———————

The man drove us to a neighborhood close to the city center. At one point in time, it probably had been a pleasant residential part of town, but it had been neglected and was now noticeably run-down. Clusters of warehouses and industrial plants encroached on what was left of the residential area, leaving behind a few isolated and forlorn-looking apartment buildings in their wake. The man drove us to one such building, a bleak two-story cement structure that hugged the ground and looked more like a bunker than an apartment complex. I could not help but notice that every window had its shades drawn, as if the people inside were sheltering themselves from the industrial onslaught around them. Or perhaps, I thought, they had something to hide.

The interior of the man's apartment did little to negate the general atmosphere of neglect and decay. It was almost completely devoid of furniture other than a shabby couch, a flat-screen TV, and several large mattresses strewn about the place as if dropped there with no care or attention at all. There were no pictures on the walls, no knickknacks or personal items, nothing to suggest that this was somebody's home. Given the expensive nature of the man's clothes and car, I immediately suspected that this apartment was some kind of hideout or sex den.

I exchanged glances with Almaz, who seemed to be thinking the same thing, but there was nothing we could do at this point, not until an opportunity presented itself.

The man never introduced himself or told us his name. Nevertheless, he spoke to us in an easy, open manner, as if we were old friends. "You are safe here, my beauties," he said, pouring us each a large glass of an unknown alcoholic beverage from the kitchen. I took a sip and almost gagged—it was very strong. I hoped the man would not make us drink it, but he prodded us repeatedly, even taking our glasses and putting them to our mouths himself. I felt light-headed even before my first glass was finished. I could see it was having an impact Almaz as well.

We settled down on the couch and continued to drink. The man seemed content to do little else. He took off his suit jacket, unbuttoned his shirt, and loosened his belt, allowing his substantial stomach to spill out over the top of his trousers. Though he was Arab, he did not dress in the traditional robe, looking and behaving like a Western man more than anything else.

He took our glasses to the kitchen and made us another drink. Almaz tried to object, but the man would not hear of it. I shot my friend a look meant to discourage her from pressing the issue, but she already seemed to understand. We both knew that if we upset our peculiar host we risked being turned over to the police. The man himself underscored this point, reminding us at regular intervals that he knew we were somehow in trouble. He warned us that we did not want to fall into the hands of the Dubai police. And while he said everything in his friendly, offhand manner, I detected an underlying threat. Clearly, we were there to have fun and drink with our new benefactor. Otherwise, it could go very badly for us.

Over the course of the afternoon, the man rambled on about a variety of topics. Eventually, however, the subject of sex began to dominate the one-sided conversation. He told us all about his sexual preferences, divulging things that, prior to my time with the Jackal, would have shocked me. As he spoke, it became clear that the apartment was a place that he and several other men rented so they could fulfill their sexual fantasies. It seemed like many women had passed through the place prior to us, undergoing all kinds of sexual ordeals, most of which revolved around bondage, dominance, and various acts of sadism.

After we had almost finished our second drink and my head was swimming, the man produced several pills from his pocket. "Take them, my beauties," he said. He claimed they would counter the effects of the alcohol and help us sleep through the night. I shot Almaz a warning look, but it was too late. My friend blithely swallowed the pills before I could stop her. I wanted to scream at her for being so stupid. How could she simply trust this strange man whose name we did not even know? If I had learned anything since my abduction, it was to always question everyone's motives, no matter who they were or how long I had known them or how much I trusted them. Suspicion was critical to survival.

As the man eyed me, I made a show of putting the pills in my mouth, trying to do so as nonchalantly as Almaz had just done. In reality, however, I cupped them in my hands and stuffed them between the couch cushions when he turned away. It was easy to fool him, I thought. But now I was unsure of my next move.

In a matter of minutes, Almaz went from looking drunk to almost completely dazed. She had trouble keeping her head up and then slumped over slightly to her side. Her hands rested on either side of her in unnatural positions. She tried to speak, but her words merged into a continuous slur that was impossible to understand. It was frightening to watch her sudden transformation.

I had to think fast. I mimicked the stages of impairment I had just witnessed Almaz go through, hoping the man did not notice how rapidly I progressed through them in order to catch up with my friend's current condition. The man, sipping his drink in eerie silence now, studied us closely but did not seem to suspect anything. Eventually, he stood up and walked into the kitchen. My mind raced as I scanned the room, looking for anything I could use as a weapon. But the apartment was so sparsely furnished that I saw nothing. As the man reentered the room,

I just barely had time to return to my slumping position and feign unconsciousness once again.

When the man returned to the kitchen for the second time, I opened my eyes and spotted a dead plant in the corner of the room. It was in a medium-sized clay pot that looked just heavy enough to make a decent weapon. If I caught the man by surprise when he emerged from the kitchen, I might be able to knock him out by smashing it over his head. It was my only chance, I thought, as I observed my friend, who was now totally unconscious and open to whatever fate the man had in store for us.

I heard the man continue to move about in the kitchen, so I stood up and quickly crossed the room. My head was spinning from the alcohol, and I felt unsteady on my feet, but my body buzzed with adrenaline. The potted plant was heavier than I expected, so I yanked out the dead plant, taking a large chunk of dirt with it, and carried the pot as quietly as possible to the kitchen doorway. Carefully positioning myself to one side, I lifted the pot high above my head with both hands and waited.

At that moment, there was a knock at the front door. My heart leapt into my throat as I realized I was on the wrong side of the doorway; the man would be turning toward me as he emerged from the kitchen to answer the door. I vaulted across the entrance to the other side but it was too late; the man appeared directly in front of me just as I was midstride. Still holding the pot above my head, I brought it down with everything I had, but it was an awkward, off-balance attempt that the man partially blocked by throwing up his arms at the last second. The pot slipped from my hands and flipped over, raining clods of dirt down on our heads before smashing to pieces on the floor between us.

I fought like a wild animal, violently kicking and punching and scratching the man, knowing that my life, as well as my friend's, depended on it. I screamed and cried out, hoping against my better judgment that whoever was on the other side of the front door might somehow help. We crossed the room as we struggled and fought each other, eventually toppling over the back of the couch and onto the floor. The man, landing on top of me, quickly took advantage of his sheer size and bulk to pin me down. He wrapped both hands around my neck and started to strangle me. I clawed at his arms and face as I choked under the intense pressure of his grip, which only tightened under my feeble efforts to break free. I felt one last spike of adrenaline and fear before the darkness closed in and I lost consciousness.

I awoke to a loud bang. Slowly opening my eyes, I tried to focus on something solid but could only make out a fuzzy, drab whiteness. Eventually, I realized that I was lying flat on my back and staring up at the ceiling. I tried to remember exactly where I was or what had happened, and for a few more moments I thought I had awoken from a deep sleep inside the back of a truck. Turning my head, I saw that I was lying at the base of a couch, and after a few more moments, I remembered where I was. Everything came flooding back in a sudden rush of awareness, and I sat up with a start and gulped for air, as if I had been drowning and had just managed to break the surface of the water.

As I gradually recovered, I took in my surroundings. Almaz and, strangely enough, another girl lay naked and passed out on the couch. Their clothes were strewn about the room. As for myself, I remained fully clothed; it seemed like I had not been touched at all. In fact, I had not even been moved from the same location where the man had choked me unconscious. Perhaps he did not want anything to do with me, I thought, after I'd demonstrated such a willingness to fight. Whatever the explanation, all I knew was that I had resisted and was not stripped naked like Almaz and this other girl. Those were the facts. It paid off to fight back.

I suddenly realized that the bang I had heard must have been the front door slamming shut. I carefully stood up and, still unsteady on my feet, cautiously searched the apartment to make sure it was empty. Then I peeked out the window. There, in the parking lot, the man was leaning against his car and speaking on his cell phone. Determined to fight back once again, I ran to the kitchen and grabbed an empty wine bottle. This time I would not fail, I told myself, as I returned to the window. But to my relief, I saw the man had climbed into his car. I watched as he exited the parking lot and drove out of sight.

Having no idea how long he would be gone, I rushed to Almaz's side and immediately tried to wake her. I shook my friend violently, causing her to stir slightly. But I could not bring her out of her stupor. I ran to the kitchen again and fetched a glass of water. I splashed it on her face and followed that up with a hard slap. Bit by bit, Almaz became conscious enough for me to lead her to the shower, where I clutched my friend as I directed a stream of cold water over her. Once she had revived enough to stand on her own, I left her and searched for her clothes. I briefly attempted to wake the other girl on the couch, but she did not even stir, and I was forced to give up. There was no way of knowing when the man would return, and I believed that in this world, at least, everyone had to fend for themselves at some point. I felt sorry for her, whoever she was, but I had to move quickly.

I took out the American's phone from the inside pocket of my pants, where I had hidden it, only to discover that the battery was dead once again. I dressed Almaz with whatever clothes I could find. After peeking out the window and scanning the parking lot again, I decided it was as good a time as any to make a break for it. It was now or never. I grabbed Almaz, who was still so dazed and unsteady that I was forced to hold her around the waist as we stumbled out the door. Fortunately, in this neighborhood, being more of an industrial area, we were less conspicuous. I also remembered that it was Sunday, which explained why the streets were so empty. Supporting Almaz, I made my way toward a cluster of tall buildings near the downtown area. I knew that if I could get close to the less glamorous sections of the city near the central business district, we had a good chance of running into a side street with nightclubs and brothels. Perhaps there we would find someone who could hide us temporarily or help us contact the twins. As we approached the city center, however, I grew increasingly nervous that we would draw more attention. We had to get as near to the area as possible without being noticed.

We staggered down a side street, moving parallel to a high brick wall surrounding a warehouse of some kind. Suddenly, a man emerged from a door directly ahead of us. Caught off guard, I froze with what must have been a look of terror on my face because the man immediately stopped and stared at us with intense curiosity. He looked at us in silence, still holding the door ajar.

I quickly appraised the man: he was older, with a neatly trimmed white beard that stood out sharply against his light-brown skin. He wore a turban and a long, flowing shirt that made me think he was a foreigner. Taking a chance, I blurted out, "Can you help us? We are not from here and are running away from a man who has drugged us and treated us very badly. He will kill us if he catches us. We are just trying to get to our friends."

The man closed the door and looked past us down the narrow street. He motioned toward a taxi parked on the opposite side. "This is my car," he said in an unfamiliar, melodic accent. "I will take you wherever you want to go."

We piled into the car, and the man passed me a cell phone. "Call your friends. Tell them you are on your way."

I knew it was best to remain quiet, but I could not help myself and asked, "Why are you helping us?"

"I have daughters," the man answered simply.

I was not able to reach the twins, so after conferring with Almaz, who was quickly recovering her mental faculties, we had the taxi driver drop us on a side street where we knew they sometimes worked their "side jobs." The street was lined with dingy nightclubs. We lingered near the entrance to one club where a group of drunken male tourists chatted up a pair of women in high heels and tight dresses. By chance, Almaz overheard a group of women speaking Amharic in the alley beside us. She approached them and learned they were just beginning a shift at the nightclub. They sympathized with their disheveled coun-trywoman and told us to wait outside the workers' entrance as they ducked inside to find someone who could help us. Twenty minutes later, a young girl emerged and spoke with Almaz. She was knocking off and said she could sneak us on a shuttle bound for a nearby labor camp; the driver would just assume we worked at the club as well. She explained that most women from Ethiopia stayed in her camp, so we would most likely find our friends there. In any case, it was as good a place to start as any.

We boarded the shuttle with little difficulty and were dropped off in the middle of what we soon discovered was Dubai's largest all-female labor camp. The area was even more bleak and disheartening than the one we had just come from: garbage was strewn about everywhere, the streets were littered with potholes, and the buildings were giant, run-down cement structures with almost no windows. Laundry hung from all the balconies and dangled from windows, adding to the well-worn appearance of the place.

The girl from the nightclub borrowed a friend's phone so we could call the twins again. After several tries, we managed to reach them. They were at work but knew everything—the entire Kassab household was abuzz with what had happened. The police had come and gone several times throughout the day. As it turned out, we were now only several blocks from the twins' flat. After several calls back and forth, we finally arranged for one of their roommates to come and fetch us.

It was dark by the time we arrived at the flat, which was located in one of the bunker-like buildings that, without a guide, would have been impossible to identify. It was as drab and disorderly inside as it was out: the tiny front room was crammed from floor to ceiling with four sets of bunk beds, the walls were unpainted cement blocks that the girls had tried to brighten up with hundreds of glossy magazine photos and advertisements, and the drop-down ceiling had collapsed in several places, exposing a mess of tangled wiring. A lonely, feeble-looking light bulb that hung down to my waist provided the only light. Like on the exterior of the building, laundry covered every inch of available space, and some girls had hung sheets in front of their beds for privacy. But what really stood out was the oppressive, sweltering heat; within minutes, I was drenched in sweat. I was relieved to learn that we had to sleep on the roof; the room was simply too small to squeeze in additional bodies. Plus, there was a possibility the police would come looking for us.

There must have been at least thirty girls sleeping on the roof. We found a spot on the far end and fashioned a makeshift bed out of a piece of tarp and some borrowed blankets. Exhausted, I immediately fell into a deep sleep the moment I hit the ground.

12

IT WAS STILL DARK when one of the twins woke us and led us past the sleeping bodies on the roof to the dusty street below, where a pack of mangy-looking dogs poked around an open pile of garbage.

"Who are all those girls on the roof?" I asked.

"Some just stay here," she answered. "It is better to sleep on the roof because the rooms are too hot." She glanced up and shrugged her shoulders. "You see there are few windows." She went on as we followed her down the street, "Some girls are runaways or illegals who have nowhere else to go. Like you now. So maybe they are looking for work in the nightclubs or tourist bars. They move from place to place."

"But where are we going now?" I asked.

"You cannot stay here," she said as she turned onto a side street. "The old lady has informed the police about you. She told them that you tried to kill her, so they will surely come looking for you here because we work together. It is a big thing."

Almaz clucked her tongue and muttered something under her breath.

Our friend continued, "They are looking for runaways and illegals now more than ever. Especially those who are said to be criminals. It has been a big thing now for the past several months. The police and *sayyad* are here now all the time."

"What is sayyad?" I asked. I felt as if I had just entered a whole new world.

"Sayyad are hunters. People who are paid to hunt illegals, especially those who are said to be dangerous. The sayyad are all over now. Sometimes they are like us—foreigners—who are paid by the police or

171

security companies. They get a little money for every runaway they find." She turned to face us now, touched Almaz lightly on the arm, and carefully repeated, "It is a big thing now with you, with what has happened. You must go to another part of town where you can hide."

We walked for several more blocks before entering an alleyway where a taxi was waiting for us. The driver, a middle-aged Indian man with a thick black beard, leaned against the car smoking a cigarette. He stood up when he saw us, nodded his head politely, and opened the door. "Please come with me," he said. "I will take you to Jebel Ali."

As we drove in the early-morning light, he glanced at us through the rearview mirror. "I am Rakesh," he said amicably. "I will take you to Jebel Ali. You should not worry; you are going to a safe place. No sayyad. And as for the police, they are all in the pockets of the D-gang. You are under their protection. So no problem, no problem."

I exchanged looks with Almaz. We had no choice but to trust this man. We remained silent as he drove us with obvious familiarity through the narrow backstreets of Dubai. I stared out the window at neighborhoods fronted by rows of grimy shops and blackened industrial sites. It was a dreary, cryptic landscape that wound its way through the city like a snake.

Seeming to read my mind, Rakesh smiled at me in the rearview mirror. "You did not expect such poor neighborhoods to be so plentiful in Dubai," he said. "The government is very good at hiding them from the tourists and their citizens." He explained how migrant labor camps in particular were built far away from the tourist areas. Most could not be found on any maps. Some camps, such as Sonapur, where Rakesh stayed—he noted with some bitterness that Sonapur translated in Hindi as "City of Gold"—were located in the desert as far as an hour out. Workers were shuttled to their jobs by 6:00 AM, where they worked eighteen-hour days before being returned late at night. Most had no idea what Dubai even looked like beyond the confines of their labor camp and jobsite and what passed before their eyes as they stared out the barred windows of the stifling buses that took them back and forth. The camps and their occupants were meant to be silent and unseen, Rakesh said. "The camps are built to contain foreign matter," he sneered. "To them, we are polluted."

Rakesh also seemed to sense my growing anxiety. He tried to reassure me. "You must trust me when I say that you are going to a safe place." He blinked and gave a small laugh. "You are not the first runaway maids in Dubai. There are many . . . thousands, maybe. I have brought many like you to Jebel Ali. This is normal. No problem." As he drove, Rakesh spoke about runaway maids and other migrant laborers—especially construction workers—and how they faced the same general problems: all were in debt to notoriously corrupt recruiting agents and moneylenders who had secured them their jobs through connections with unsympathetic employers whose power was reinforced by the kafala system. He described it as a form of debt bondage, which included a string of overseas recruiters and moneylenders who were in lockstep with local employers, or sponsors. Between trying to repay their loans, which quickly grew out of hand, and sending money back home to family members, Dubai's foreign workers barely survived. Meanwhile, they were exposed to a barrage of exploitative labor practices and dangerous work conditions. Many individuals decided it was better to simply abscond and survive as an illegal than to work within an underhanded system specifically set up to ensure their continued indebtedness. "This is how they treat the people who clean and build their city," Rakesh concluded with bitterness.

Almaz, who had seemed lost in her thoughts all morning, suddenly leaned forward. "We are from Africa," she said. "We want to go home. Can you help us get home?"

Rakesh paused before answering. "I cannot help you myself, no. Maybe you can work a deal with the D-gang. I cannot say."

"Who is this D-gang?" Almaz asked.

"They run things in Jebel Ali. But they are not . . . official. For you, because you are illegals who maybe have trouble, it is a good place to go."

Listening to Rakesh, I could not help but be reminded of the 28 and wondered if I was simply continuing a pattern of climbing out of one hole only to fall into another. It gave me a sick, sinking feeling.

Rakesh drove to the edge of Dubai, where the somber-looking remnants of the city buffeted the desert. He left the road and followed a dirt path that skirted a row of graffitied apartment buildings. On our left, the desert sands stretched to the horizon. Plastic bags and other bits of garbage blew about in small corkscrews of swirling dust. Here and there, piles of empty beer cans and liquor bottles dotted the vast landscape. Rakesh drove gingerly over the rutted path, pausing at each narrow alleyway as it sliced into the faded buildings at regular intervals. Finally, he stopped in front of one opening and turned off the car. "We are here," he said.

A slight and very pretty black woman in a pink dress and headscarf materialized from a doorway in the alley. She tottered toward us clasping a bucket of water before emptying its contents on the ground. Turning her attention to us, she said in a wispy voice, "I am Waris. You are welcome."

"Go with her now," said Rakesh. "It is OK. No problem." He caught my eye and smiled. "I can come and visit you, OK?" I smiled and nodded absentmindedly.

Rakesh left us with Waris, who stood before us still clutching her bucket. She seemed to appraise us for a moment before gesturing toward the desert. "This is the Big Ground," she said. "It is a place where the men come to drink after work. They come from all the camps around here. There are many." She turned and motioned for us to follow her back into the alley. "You are welcome," she repeated softly.

She led us into the building from where she had just come, passing down a few steps and into a narrow hallway constructed of bits and pieces of cardboard attached to scrap metal and chicken wire. The only light came from a series of dingy yellow bulbs that dangled from wires in random places, which gave the entire place a murky, dungeon-like appearance. A smattering of empty bottles and cans lay about the floor, as if blown in by the desert winds like the small drifts of sand that massed just inside the doorway. The smell of raw sewage hung in the air. Somewhere in the darkness somebody was cooking meat. The sweet, acrid smell, which I normally found inviting, now made me want to vomit. We passed a series of narrow doorways, most of which were covered by a towel or strip of cloth. Those that were left uncovered revealed small groups of young women and girls sitting on the floor. I noticed that they all had black or brown skin. They stared up at us with vacant expressions when we passed.

Waris led us around a corner and through an open doorway into one of the side rooms. Like most, it was windowless and contained young women, in this case two girls who were squatting over a small cookstove on the floor. Other than several crude sleeping mats, the room was empty. Newspaper covered the walls except the back one, which was made from cinder blocks and appeared to be original rather than the improvised construction that characterized the rest of the place.

The two occupants were from a town in Ethiopia near Addis Ababa. Almaz spoke to them for a long time in Amharic before passing on what she learned. She confirmed that we were in a place where men—mostly from India—came to drink after work. They gathered on the desert plain just outside, or what Waris had referred to as the Big Ground. The Big Ground was a place where large amounts of alcohol were available, including an especially strong concoction called *tharra*, which the girls sold from the building we were in now. After a glass or two of tharra, most men wanted sex, and the girls were there to oblige them. "Everything here is just about alcohol and sex," Almaz said. "And the men who make money from it. They are part of this D-gang." She said that a constant procession of girls cycled through the building as they moved between the Big Ground and bars or nightclubs or found work as domestic servants. Many were runaways like us, or what were officially known as "absconders," while others did not have a legal visa to stay in the UAE, either because their previous employer did not return it for some reason, they had lost it, or they simply never had one to begin with. Almaz clucked her tongue and said, "Every girl has her story of suffering."

"But what if we just want to go home?" I asked, dreading the thought of an existence based on selling alcohol and sex in such an awful place.

"I have told them about our situation and our wish to return home," Almaz answered. "But these girls say it is better to stay quiet and out of sight. And then we might have time to think about it. They say if the old lady goes to the police, then we must remain here; it is the best place to hide." Almaz studied her hands as she considered our situation. "I, too, would like to go home now," she said softly. "But I think we should stay here for now. With God's blessing we will find an opportunity to return to Africa together."

Later that evening, the Big Ground sprang to life. First, men came through the building distributing bottles of tharra, which our new roommates warned us not to drink. If we did, they said, we would almost immediately get sick. They claimed it took a long time for a person to build up their tolerance to tharra; it was extremely dangerous to drink more than a few sips at first. In any case, the girls were forbidden to drink it, and even when it was sold to men it was doled out in carefully measured amounts. Girls who were found drunk or with alcohol on their breath were beaten. I noticed a group of intimidating bouncers who seemed perfectly capable of carrying out such punishments. While there were no identifiable leaders among the so-called D-gang, there was an obvious force behind the whole operation.

Later in the evening, we learned that we were "to go on parade," an activity that entailed joining one of a number of groups—all girls—who walked among the men as they gathered on the Big Ground. Our roommates assured us that all we had to do was walk around, make eye contact, and smile. Everybody knew who we were and why we were there.

Waris came for us when it was our turn to go on parade. We followed her outside, where I was astonished to see hundreds of men scattered about the previously desolate desert plain. They were all talking and laughing as they mingled about, some still in their work clothes. Everyone was drinking openly. A nearby group huddled together on the ground, playing a game on a crude board made of cloth. Here and there, hawkers sold nuts, eggs, bread, fruit, and fish, displaying their wares in neat little piles on blankets spread on the ground. I thought the entire scene looked like some kind of traditional gathering for men.

Our little parade group consisted of myself, Almaz, Waris, and three other girls. We wove in and out among the men as we strolled around the Big Ground. A sea of eyes fell upon us, and Waris reminded us to smile and make simple greetings.

"These men are all from India," Waris said in her soft, almost silky voice. "They are all lonely. Alcohol and women are an escape from their lonely lives—if they have money." She told us to be on the lookout for men who were suicidal, explaining that so many killed themselves that the Indian embassy had found it necessary to establish a hotline for them. "Please remind me to give you the number when we return from parade," Waris said, as she floated like a specter between the men. "You will need it."

We worked our way along the row of buildings bordering the Big Ground until we turned onto a paved road, where we were confronted by rows of buses parked outside a small food shop. Two long lines of men ran parallel to the buses, waiting to purchase either beer or whiskey. A man stood on top of one bus and shouted out, "This queue is for beer! This queue is for whiskey!" Other men were busy hauling boxes of alcohol from the buses to the front of each line. I noticed again how efficiently things were run.

The man on the bus spotted us and called out, "Brothers! I think you know that these women are selling plenty of tharra." His announcement elicited a low rumble of laughter.

Waris turned her delicate frame and smiled. "You see, here tharra is more than just tharra." She led us past the lines of men one more time before returning us to our building.

Rakesh the taxi driver was waiting in the alleyway. He approached me and said quietly, "I have money for tharra."

Waris laughed breezily. "Very good," she said, ushering us inside.

Rakesh visited frequently over the next month as I settled into my new life as a Big Ground girl. I liked Rakesh; he was polite and soft-spoken, even to the point of being shy. Sometimes he did not even want sex, preferring instead to sip his tharra, smoke cigarettes, and talk, mostly about his problems back in India. Parts of his story were familiar to me; I heard them again and again from every man who visited me: growing debts back home, problems with banks and moneylenders, suspicions about wives and girlfriends, and endless problems with employers in Dubai. And underlying everything was a potent mix of shame, frustration, and bitterness. After only one month at the Big Ground, I felt as if I could have written each man's story. But Rakesh's problems seemed to haunt him more than most.

The life of a Big Ground girl was a simple one: to sell as much sex and alcohol as possible to an army of lonely and troubled men. They gathered on the Big Ground every evening after work, with the largest crowds forming on Thursdays, Fridays, and Saturdays, but there were men on the Big Ground almost every evening. The entire operation was run by the mysterious D-gang, whose authority was reflected in day-to-day operations and the extensive network of men on the ground, each of whom had a specific role: vendors sold the alcohol, spokers marketed it, transporters—usually taxi drivers and bus drivers—delivered it, stashers cached and concealed it, spotters acted as lookouts, foodies sold food, and fixers negotiated with the police through an elaborate system of bribes.

Girls were an essential part of this world. We were managed by a large and resourceful Kenyan lady known only as Queen Victoria. At any given time, the Queen oversaw between seventy-five and one hundred girls at the Big Ground brothel. Girls came and went, but the Queen remained a constant presence. Nobody knew for sure how long she had been there, but it was long enough for her to know everything about the Big Ground.

The Queen also had considerable influence over the tharra business, a product she absolutely forbade us from drinking. She once warned me that it was made in part from radiator fluid and that a few men died each year from drinking it. I believed her; the men's breath always had a gasoline-like odor—even after one small glass. The smell was so strong that I often felt dizzy myself whenever a man, drunk from tharra, pawed and panted over me. One time, I had to turn my head and vomit as a drunken construction worker lay on top of me. He did not seem to mind, however, and simply continued to force himself on me, breathing and snorting the heavy tharra fumes in my face.

But the darkest part of the Big Ground activities occurred on Thursday and Friday nights, when groups of young boys were bussed in to satisfy the sexual appetites of a surprising number of men. The boys, most of whom looked to be under thirteen, were delivered early, before the crowds gathered, and immediately ushered to the top floor of the building. One girl told me that they were shipped in from Somalia just for this purpose. The "boy deli," as it was known around the brothel, was never discussed in much detail, but like the Big Ground itself, it was an open secret.

Rakesh continued to act as an intermediary for Almaz and me between the Big Ground and the outside world, relaying information from the

twins regarding our situation. It was serious; the police were actively looking for us after Madame Dua's accusations of attempted murder. In several
parts of the city, flyers with our photos were distributed to shopkeepers and
nightclub owners. A local newspaper highlighted the incident in its crime
section, and the story was picked up by other media outlets. It included
an interview with Madam Dua, who claimed we were practicing witches
and HIV positive, among other things. The entire episode contributed
to a crackdown on absconders and domestic workers who were in the
country illegally. While plenty of girls who passed through the doors of
the Big Ground brothel had run away from their domestic service jobs,
few were on the police's radar to such a degree or had an accuser as earnest
as Madam Dua. Given all the attention, Rakesh advised us to stay put.

I kept the American's cell phone with me at all times, never letting
it out of my sight. Almaz thought it was too risky to try anything for
the time being and advised me to just hold on to it. But I was growing increasingly unhappy with our situation—much more so than my
friend—and was desperate to find a way out of Dubai. I could never
get used to this kind of life. So I decided to confide in Rakesh about
the stolen phone.

Rakesh examined the phone as I told him the story behind it. When I
came to the part involving the video, Rakesh held up a hand. "There is no
need to tell me or for me to see this video," he said reassuringly. "Besides,"
he continued. "There are other videos with other girls. This man has a
large appetite." Rakesh scrolled carefully through the American's e-mails
as he smoked his cigarette and sipped his tharra. Finally, he looked up
and said, "This is an important man."

"What should I do? Can you help me?" I asked anxiously.

"I must do some more looking into this man first," Rakesh answered.
"But yes, I think I can help you. No problem. You have something over
this man, and maybe you can use it. It could hurt him very much. But
you must be very careful. I will help you." Rakesh studied a photo of
the American and his family standing in front of a large, beautiful house.
He said quietly, almost as if to himself, "It is everything a man wants."
He stared at the photo for a long time, but to me his eyes seemed to be
looking at something far away.

The following week, Rakesh came back to me with news about the American. He confirmed that the man was very high up in the UN World Food Programme. "Higher than we thought," he said. "He is a powerful man who meets regularly with Dubai's political leaders. This man has much to lose. I have found out who his bosses are. And he has a big family back in America too. I think he would be ruined if people saw the videos on this phone."

Our plan was simple: We would send an e-mail to the man demanding enough money for me to get home and Rakesh to pay off his debts. If he did not comply, we would send the video to everyone on his contact list, including his family and his work colleagues. We would also tell him that we knew about the other damaging videos on his phone and were prepared to send those out as well. To prove that we had his phone and were serious, we would attach still photos from several of the videos.

"We must also make copies of everything," Rakesh said. "Just in case." He asked if he could take the phone to an acquaintance who could back up the files and send the e-mail.

I hesitated. I had never allowed the phone to leave my sight. But I trusted my instincts when it came to people now, a trait that had been tested and honed over the past couple of years. And there was something about Rakesh that told me he could be trusted. I gave him the phone.

Rakesh returned the phone the next day. "It is done," he said. "Now we must wait." He laughed and added, "At least you know that you can trust me now."

———

As I spent time with Rakesh, I learned more details about his life and how he came to Dubai. He told me that he had a fiancée back in India, in his home state of Kerala. Her name was Nishi, and he had known her all his life; he loved her very much and often described the time he spent with her as his only real joy. They had grown up together in the same village, played together, schooled together, and made their plans for the future knowing that they would always be by each other's side. As teenagers, they had often walked along the banks of the Periyar River, chatting endlessly about their lives and dreams for the future.

For Rakesh to make his plans with Nishi a reality, he needed to purchase a large plot of land. His prospective father-in-law insisted on it before paying the dowry and giving his daughter away. But Rakesh came from a family with four older brothers, and his parents were not well off, so inheriting land of his own was out of the question. He would have to find a way to make his own fortune. And like so many men from his village who faced similar circumstances, that meant finding work in Dubai. So Rakesh secured a loan from the bank and paid a local recruiter to find him his Dubai job. The lending conditions were severe, but, as Rakesh told me, at least he did not borrow money from the "blade mafia," so called because of their cutthroat rates and violent enforcement strategies. As for the recruiter, his fees were substantial, but he assured Rakesh that he could pay off the loan within two years, buy a nice plot of land, and even have enough money left over to open up a small shop. This sounded perfect, so Rakesh committed himself to two years of hard work in Dubai, knowing that it would enable him to finally begin his dream life with Nishi. The recruiter congratulated him on his wise decision.

Like so many men from his area, Rakesh harbored dreams of becoming a "Gulfan man," a popular reference to those lucky Gulf migrants who hit it big and returned home fabulously wealthy. In his quiet manner, he explained to me just how powerful and alluring the image of the Gulfan man was back in his home village: it was widely promoted in Indian films and plays, told and retold in stories, and referenced countless times in everyday conversation. "As a Gulfan," Rakesh explained to me once, "I would return home with gifts for everybody. I would be wearing designer shirts and gold watches and very expensive sunglasses. I would smoke American cigarettes and drive a nice car." He closed his eyes, as if trying to imagine himself what that might look like. "Yesss," he cooed dreamily, "I would make a very good Gulfan." He explained how the image of the Gulfan man represented the aspirations of so many young men from his area that the very act of migrating to the Gulf and striking it big was now considered a necessary step toward becoming a full-fledged man.

But upon arriving in Dubai, things went downhill for Rakesh right from the start. The construction company that hired him had been withholding wages from its workers for over six weeks, which led to a general strike among the men. Rakesh, who had only been there for four weeks when the strike began, had not received even his first paycheck. Things only got worse as tensions escalated. The company, in retaliation against its striking employees, canceled their work visas, refused to return their passports, and turned off the power and water to the labor camp. The place quickly degenerated into an open cesspit of garbage and raw sewage, causing the rat population to explode until they were literally dropping from holes in the ceiling and onto the men's heads as they slept. The police were called in on several occasions and arbitrarily arrested whole groups of individuals at a time. They were brought to the police station and systematically beaten until they identified their ringleaders.

Workers began abandoning the camp after a few weeks. Rakesh joined one group and eventually ended up living in a makeshift cardboard camp in the desert almost three miles outside of Dubai. There was no point in returning home since he would never find a job in Kerala that would allow him to repay the bank loan. Besides, he explained to me, he would be returning as the village failure, a prospect so shameful that he could not imagine facing Nishi, let alone his family and friends, all of whom had such high expectations for him. In fact, returning home as anything other than a Gulfan man was considered such a sign of abject failure that it was shameful not only for the man but for his entire family as well. And the stereotype of the *failed* Gulf migrant was almost as prevalent as that of the successful one. "Gulf victims" were the pathetic figures who could not support their families, buy drinks for their friends at the neighborhood bar, put up money for a dowry, or pay off their bank loans. For many, the only option was to borrow money and go deeper into debt in order to return to the Gulf. Doing so offered them one more chance to make it big while escaping their problems at home. As Rakesh explained, that was why so many men from Kerala migrated again and again to Dubai, engaging in an endless cycle of long stints in the Middle East punctuated by brief stays back home. For these individuals, the image of the Gulfan man existed only to mock them. It became the measuring stick by which to assess their failure as men.

Eventually, Rakesh managed to find a job as a taxi driver. His taxi was part of a fleet controlled by the D-gang, who also used their vehicles to haul alcohol, cigarettes, and a few other goods. Since Rakesh did not have a work visa or even a passport at this point, it was one of the few jobs available to him. But the pay was only a fraction of what he would have made as a construction worker.

"So, here I am," Rakesh sighed in conclusion one night, as he leaned against the back wall of my room. He took a long drag from his cigarette and flashed a weak smile. "I have been driving a taxi now for three years. And what do I have to show for it? I am deeper in debt than I have ever been. I cannot go home like this. I would shame my family." He stared blankly ahead and exhaled. "I would shame Nishi," he said emptily, his eyes fixed on the opposite wall as if he were watching another, happier life unfold there. "So here I am," he repeated.

I was beginning to worry; it had been a week, and I had not seen or heard from Rakesh. He usually visited the brothel a few times a week, and on each occasion he never failed to greet me. I wondered if the American had somehow used his power and influence to find him. My mind raced through all the possible scenarios.

Finally, I approached another taxi driver—a man I recognized as a friend of Rakesh's—and asked him if he had any news on his whereabouts. The man cocked his head and studied me. "You are his friend from Africa, yes?" I nodded my head as the man fumbled around in his pockets and took out a folded envelope. He presented it to me with a strange, self-conscious look and said flatly, "Rakesh is dead . . . by his own hand. He hanged himself." I stared at the man in shock, who gestured toward the envelope I held in my hands. "He wrote that letter to you." He paused before adding, "He also wrote a letter to his mother and father and to his . . . woman . . . in India."

In the letter, Rakesh apologized for not being able to help me more. But he had sent the e-mail to the American and provided me with the username and password to the account. He acknowledged that we were both living lives we did not want or desire, but he believed my situation was different because I was young and smart and had a real opportunity to change my life. Toward that end, he encouraged me not to be afraid to force the American's hand. He had faith that my future would be full of freedom and joy one day. As for his own future, there was no hope; Nishi had written him and informed him that she was engaged to be married. It was the last straw. He ended by writing, "I don't blame her for this. There are stronger forces in the world that prevent men like me from achieving my dreams. But how does a man cast blame on these things? How do I fight these things? But they are there and there is nothing more I can do. I am sorry."

13

Since arriving at the Big Ground, Almaz had been having second thoughts about returning home to Ethiopia. If she went back, she knew it would be difficult to earn enough money to support her children in the manner she wanted, so doubts and uncertainties slowly crept back into her mind. Like so many women who ended up at the Big Ground brothel, she began to see the place as a temporary shelter until she could find another, better-paying job in Dubai. She was thinking of sharing a flat with several other ladies from Ethiopia and finding work in one of the nightclubs that catered to foreign tourists. I noticed that many girls, once they became used to the surroundings at the brothel, began networking with one another and making plans to work in Dubai's nightclub scene, which was thought to be a step up from the Big Ground brothel and its more modest clientele.

But things changed for Almaz one evening after one of our parade sessions. It was getting dark, and she lingered behind to talk with an Indian man who promised her a big tip after flashing an unusually large amount of cash in her face. He seemed like any other worker from the Big Ground but insisted on having sex at his place, which he claimed was just around the corner. Eyeing the wad of cash, Almaz could not resist. Tips, which were rare to begin with, were typically handed over to Queen Victoria. In this case, however, Almaz planned to keep the cash for herself. It was against the rules for girls to go off by themselves with any man, but she reasoned that if this one lived right around the corner, as he claimed, then she could have sex, collect the money, and be back at the brothel before anyone noticed.

As they walked together down the alley to the man's apartment, he stopped and turned toward Almaz. Thinking he wanted to kiss her, she also paused and faced the man. But before she knew what was happening, the man swung his arm up and punched her in the face. She fell to the ground, dazed, staring up at her attacker as he towered above her, fists clenched, poised to strike again. Thinking quickly, Almaz closed her eyes and turned her head, feigning unconsciousness. She could feel the blood trickling down her cheeks and into her mouth. She suspected her nose was broken. She must have looked in bad shape because the man stepped away to make a call on his cell phone.

Realizing it was her only chance, Almaz sprang up and made a mad dash down the alleyway toward the Big Ground. The man immediately gave chase and caught up to her at the intersection of a cross alley. Grabbing her by the hair, he yanked her back so violently that she stumbled and fell again. She put her arms up to protect herself from another blow, but it never came. Instead, an enormous man appeared from behind her attacker and struck him on the back of the head with a pipe. He dropped to the ground like a rock. The man with the pipe seemed to consider hitting him again but settled on kicking him in the face, sending several teeth skittering across the alley.

A whistle came from above. It was one of the D-gang spotters who positioned themselves on the rooftops to keep an eye out for police or anything out of the ordinary. He waved at the man with the pipe, who acknowledged him with a nod. Almaz recognized the big man now; he was part of the D-gang's security contingent, an imposing group of Punjabi who were rumored to be ex-military and roamed the Big Ground like ravenous tigers. Fortunately for Almaz, they had watched the entire incident unfold from the beginning; few things happened on the Big Ground without the D-gang's knowledge.

Later that night, we learned that Almaz's attacker was part of the sayyad. He confessed that he was specifically looking for the two of us, lured by the large reward. While the secretive leaders of the D-gang did not necessarily care about the fate of two African girls, they took incursions into their territory very seriously. Rumor had it that after the man was beaten and confessed to everything, he was taken deep into the desert and buried alive. It was typical of the punishments meted out to those unfortunate individuals who violated the rules of the Big Ground.

After the attack, Almaz decided to return to Ethiopia, at least for the time being. "I am no good to my children dead or in jail," she told me. "And maybe we can find a way to open a shop together in my country. Maybe Ethiopia can be your new home." I considered the idea once again. It sounded more tempting to me now, especially since I had already been thinking about Rakesh's words about bringing shame to himself and his family, which also made an impact on me. I understood that kind of pressure and realized that escaping Dubai did not necessarily mean having to return home to Namibia. I wondered if I even had a home to return to. Whenever I allowed myself to think about my life and what it might look like if I ever made it back to Namibia, I was nagged with suspicion and doubt about my family and their failure to protect me on the day of my abduction. That led, in turn, to the one question that haunted me: Did my uncle—and, more importantly, my father—know beforehand that I was to be abducted? I could not bear to think about it.

After discussing our options, Almaz and I agreed to approach Queen Victoria for help. She was one of the few people who could help us: she was not only street savvy but also plugged in to Dubai's underground network of gang members, scammers, smugglers, and sex workers—a definite asset when it came to things like blackmailing rich Americans. At the same time, she had a soft heart and somehow managed to move among all these people with a doting, almost motherly affection, especially when it came to "her girls" at the Big Ground brothel. She may have played the role of a sympathetic nursemaid, but few doubted the Queen's ability to slit a man's throat when necessary. She was perfect.

We decided our best bet was to be honest and appeal to the Queen's sense of decency by telling her the full story, including the entire odyssey of my abduction and how I had come to Dubai. One evening, the Queen invited us to her room and, after closing and locking the door, listened quietly to our story, interjecting only to ask a few questions. On several occasions, she looked at me with shock and exclaimed, "Oh, you poor dear!" When I was finished, the Queen took my hands in hers and said, "I am feeling pity for you, my daughter. I truly am." She then leaned back and thought for a while before asking how much money we were demanding from the American and whether he had responded. I told her the amount, admitting that I had not checked for a response in several days.

"Oh! Let us see, then!" the Queen boomed, pulling out an iPad from among the voluminous folds of her robe. We quickly confirmed that the American had not responded, even though it had been over a week.

"Sometimes you must give such things time to work on a man," the Queen said reassuringly. "Even the moon and the sun move slowly, but eventually they cross the sky." She turned her attention to Rakesh's e-mail and nodded her head. "Ah, yes, this is good. I will help you. But you must give me this man's share of the money now. Do you agree to this?" We exchanged glances and quickly agreed. The Queen continued, "And we must double the amount we want from this man. You are thinking too small. He is an American, after all, and I am certain this is nothing to him." She noted how the original message did not take Almaz into account, so asking for more money would ensure that she could return home as well. Putting down the iPad, the Queen slapped her hands on her knees. "Now!" she said. "Give me this American's phone. Let us see if we can put more meat in the trap!"

———

The American had still not responded by the end of the week, so Queen Victoria sent several more e-mails. I asked to read them, but the Queen simply laughed, patted me on the shoulder, and told me not to worry, assuring me that he would reply, probably very soon.

The very next evening, the Queen intercepted us as we were about to go on parade. "There has been a response," she whispered excitedly. "Come with me."

We followed Queen Victoria to her room, where she went through the same routine of carefully shutting and locking the door before settling down and beginning to speak. "He has agreed to our demands," she said, beaming. "But he says it will be difficult to put you on a plane when you do not have passports and are wanted by the police. I do not know how he knows these things." Almaz suggested that he may have been in contact with the Kassab family and Madam Dua; it was the most likely explanation. "Well, it is no matter," the Queen continued, "because the American has offered a solution." She explained that he would put us on a World Food Programme flight to Addis Ababa. Once in Ethiopia, I would have to find my own way back to Namibia, but the amount of cash he was giving me would be enough to make that possible. "So that is the deal," the Queen said, spreading her arms.

Trusting so few people these days, I asked skeptically, "How do we know this is not a trap?"

But Queen Victoria had a plan: We would go to the airport together, and once there, the American himself would ensure that we were safely on the plane. Several D-gang members would accompany us as security, and she would only return the man's phone once the plane was in the air. The American was aware that she had copies of everything. "And there are other things I can use as leverage with this man," the Queen said mysteriously. "I do not think there will be any problems."

On the day we were scheduled to depart, the American was waiting for us in a shopping mall parking lot near the airport. We remained in the car with a D-gang security guard while Queen Victoria and a second guard, who happened to be the pipe-wielding man who had disposed of Almaz's attacker, approached the American's car. When he rolled down his window to speak with the Queen, we confirmed that it was Mike the American. I could never forget that soft, pale face. I knew now it was the face of a man who had as much to lose as he had to hide.

After a brief discussion, the Queen returned to our car, and we followed the American to the airport, where he used his World Food Programme credentials to get us through a special entrance to the airport's Humanitarian

Response Depot. "He is alone, and he is nervous," Queen Victoria said. "When such a man is alone and nervous, it is always a good sign."

We passed through the security checkpoint with surprising ease; the guards simply waved us through after exchanging a few words with the American. They appeared to know him, and one guard even made a small, respectful bow as he went by. Once inside, we passed row upon row of large warehouses, all identical, with blue roofs and white corrugated metal walls that shimmered brightly in the afternoon sun. Forklifts and other vehicles scurried between the buildings and several massive cargo planes on the tarmac. Every plane had WFP painted in large, blue letters on its tail.

We parked in front of one warehouse, and the Queen, accompanied by both security guards this time, followed the American inside. Several minutes later, she emerged carrying a plastic bag, climbed back into the car, and said with a broad smile, "It is good. You will be back in the motherland today, praise be to God." She then handed Almaz and me each $1,000 in cash, in American currency. We gasped; it was more money than either of us had ever seen in our lives. "It would take several years to save up this much money working in Dubai," Almaz gushed. "This is all I need to open a shop in Ethiopia." She beamed with excitement through a pair of black eyes, the result of the broken nose suffered during the attack almost two weeks ago.

Dumbstruck, I stared at the wad of money in my hands. My mind raced through all the possible things I could do, all the opportunities for a brand-new start. At the same time, I knew it would never erase everything I had been through. In that sense, I might as well be holding a handful of ashes.

"The American will put you on the plane himself," the Queen informed us. "But you must go now."

It was all happening so quickly that I could think of nothing to say beyond a simple "Thank you."

The Queen laughed. "This is not the first time I have caught a big man in one of my traps," she said. "It will not be the last." She lifted the bag with her share of the money. "I have been blessed, my dear." She then offered me one of her caring, maternal looks and said, "You do not belong here, my dear. I have known this from the beginning. Africa is your full-time home. And with God's blessing, when Africa is under your feet again, everything will be better for you. You will be healed."

The American walked up as we were saying our goodbyes. "Follow me," he said curtly as he brushed past us toward the largest of the planes. We trailed behind him as he led us up a ramp and into a cavernous cargo hold. The interior of the plane was filled with pallets of rice and boxes labeled with the words HIGH ENERGY BISCUITS. Several workers were strapping down the last of the pallets. They glanced at us with mild curiosity but remained silent.

The American guided us to a row of jump seats lining the side of the plane. He demonstrated how to buckle ourselves in and produced a pair of headsets, which he explained were meant to deaden the noise during flight. He was all business as he strapped us in. It was as if we were just two more sacks of rice being delivered to Africa.

Taking note of the man's detached, almost haughty demeanor, Almaz clucked her tongue in disgust and scowled menacingly at him. It seemed to break the American's stony facade, which in turn sparked something deep inside me.

"I am not your dog to do with as you wish," I hissed in an icy whisper that startled even myself. I glared at the man and pounded my chest with a clenched fist. "I am a girl," I stated. But thinking this did not sound quite right, I corrected myself and practically shouted, "I am a Himba woman!" As the words came out of my mouth, I felt my grandfather's presence; I knew the Old One was sitting beside me now, leaning on his walking stick, smiling with approval.

The American gave a small start. He looked dazed, as if he, too, were seeing a ghost. I imagined it was not a position he was used to being in. He turned away and muttered sheepishly under his breath, "You will be taking off to Addis in about an hour." Only then, as I watched him retreat down the cargo ramp and out of sight, did I know for certain that I was returning to Africa. It had been two years since I was abducted.

Time passed quickly once we were back in Africa, as if making up for the slow, torturous pace at which it had been moving for the past couple of years. Before I knew it, I had been in Ethiopia for well over a year. I had grown fond of Addis Ababa, the capital city nestled high in the Ethiopian highlands at the foot of Mount Entoto. Its pleasant climate and crisp, thin air was a welcome relief from Dubai's oppressive heat. Each morning, I watched the city teem with life as its broad avenues and countless monument-filled squares filled up with people from all walks of life and every corner of Africa. The city seemed to embrace its own frenzied logic and reason for being. To me, it was as if a single bee from every hive in the land had been placed together in a giant gourd and, by some stroke of luck, had managed to produce the most wonderful honey. And the energy from this African patchwork buzzed and echoed against a backdrop that had something undeniably ancient and mystical about it. It felt like the ancestors walked among us here.

With the money she received from the American, Almaz opened a shop in the Addis Mercato, the city's labyrinthine open-air market, selling vegetables from her uncle's farm on one side and making coffee and samosas on the other. I loved to watch her make coffee—she brewed it in the traditional manner using clay vessels called jebena. She did it with as much care and attention as if she were painting a picture or carving some beautiful piece of artwork each and every day. Her clientele, consisting mostly of older men, sat for hours on rickety plastic chairs, sipping their coffee and passing the day in animated conversation. They flirted regularly with Almaz, whose skills at seducing and enchanting her fellow countrymen were on full display.

I invested part of my money in my friend's business and kept myself busy helping her to run it. Customers flirted with me as well, and I knew they watched me as I moved about the shop. But after everything I had been through, I felt their advances were harmless, mostly because they lacked the predatory bloodthirst of every man I had been with during my abduction. The men of the Mercato were just normal men with everyday desires. It was nice to be an attractive yet ordinary woman going about my business in a more manageable world.

My favorite time of day was when Almaz's two boys came rushing into the shop after school. Their mother, always ready with a long list of chores for them to do, usually sent them to some far corner of the Mercato to buy milk or sugar or anything else to keep them busy. I often joined them on these missions; I loved exploring the market and its tangled web of narrow dirt corridors and tin stalls. Its merchants sold an amazing assortment of fruits and vegetables, many of which I had never seen before. Also on display were beautifully colored fabrics, intricate handwoven baskets, burnished jewelry, strange religious relics, and so much more. The air was pungent with the aroma of incense, spice, coffee, and meat. I felt as if all of life had been squeezed and wedged into a single place. Leading me through the mayhem, Almaz's boys spent most of their time scouring the market for sweets to buy with the extra coins their mother gave them. It was all so different from the rigid order and artificial landscape of Dubai. I took it all in, knowing that it was restorative. As I wandered the market each day, I felt as if I was becoming whole again.

But I was still plagued by the witch doctor's curse. So after months of deliberation, I asked Almaz to set up a meeting with a well-known healer in Addis. The healer, a wizened old man with kind eyes and an easy, pleasant manner, reminded me of my grandfather and immediately put me at ease. As I told him the entire story of my witching, he closed his eyes and listened intently. I started from the very beginning and described everything leading up to the actual night of the witching itself. When I came to that particular night, I tried to remember every detail: the general surroundings, the people present, the murder of the young girl, the beat of the drums, the potion we were made to drink, the strange orbs of light—everything. I showed the healer the scar on the back of my arm, which he examined closely, running his heavily calloused fingertips over the wavy line, tracing it exactly, and lightly touching the three dots as if trying to divine some hidden code. He asked many questions and had me repeat certain parts of the story again and again, showing particular interest in the ingredients that were added to the potion. Finally, drawing a deep breath, he said, "I can remove this. But it will take time, maybe a month.

I must prepare something special for you each week for four weeks. It must follow your menstrual cycle. And you must also pray every day during this time. Go to church as often as you can—every day, if possible—and pray there. This, plus the medicine I give you, will heal you and remove the curse."

I followed the healer's advice to the letter, never missing a day to pray at church and visiting him every week to receive a new batch of medicine. It was a syrupy, heavily spiced drink that left me feeling invigorated. On my final visit, the healer examined me thoroughly and informed me that I was fully healed with one small exception. "You are holding something against a close family member," he said, to my surprise. "It is preventing you from moving forward with your own life. You are healed, but you are stuck—you cannot move forward or backward—you are in a nowhere place. You must confront this person and forgive them. Then you can move forward."

I knew immediately who he was referring to: my father. I was carrying something against him that I had been trying not to think about, pushing it away each time it threatened to surface. Until now, when the healer finally put it into words, I had never been willing or able to confront it.

I knew that in many ways I blamed my father for everything that had happened to me. Deep down, I think I also knew that he had no prior knowledge of or hand in my abduction. I could not say the same thing for my uncle Gerson. But I did not particularly care about my uncle. I cared only about my father. I loved him. I think that was why I resented him: because even if he could not have known the consequences of his actions on that day, he still gave up his only daughter to a man he did not even know. And for what? A few cows? It was that initial decision that led to everything else. Looking back now, I felt that at that moment on that particular day my father had had a choice, and he had chosen to hand over his daughter rather than to do something—anything—to protect and defend her. But then I asked myself: What could he possibly have done? What choices did he have on that remote desert farm in Angola almost three years ago now? It was difficult to think of anything he could have done, given the forces aligned against us. And I realized that those forces were simply too powerful and immense for one Himba family from the

Kunene to control or even understand. No, it was foolish to blame my father. The healer was right; I must forgive him to completely heal and move forward with my life.

———————

Several more months passed before I was ready to call home. Initially, I phoned a cousin my age who lived in Opuwo and asked her to tell my parents that I was alive and well. My parents were at the farm, where cell phone reception was poor, so I asked my cousin to get word to them and have them come to town as soon as possible. I told her to inform only my parents; I did not want anyone else to know where I was at the moment, especially my uncle Gerson. His close relationship with the man called Angel made me suspicious of him the most. It was difficult to have such doubts and misgivings about close family members, but that was my reality now.

When I was certain my parents were in Opuwo, I phoned again. I spoke with my mother first, who wept into the phone so uncontrollably that it took a long time before I could even understand her. Eventually, my mother described how they had tried to find out what happened to me. First, they reported me missing to the Namibian police. But the police asked a lot of questions about why they were in Angola in the first place. The government was in the midst of a crackdown on cattle rustling and illegal cross-border traffic with Angola, which made my parents fear that they, or perhaps Gerson, would get into serious trouble. So my father decided to take matters into his own hands and returned to Angola himself, carefully retracing our previous route until he found the farm where I had been taken. But his presence quickly aroused suspicions among the locals, and they reported him to the Angolan police. He was detained for several days before being loaded onto a truck and taken back to the border, where he was unceremoniously dumped with Namibian immigration officials. After that, there was little they could do but pray.

After hearing what my mother had to say, I agreed to speak with my father. He listened in silence as I recounted my story to him. I wanted to interpret his silence as shock, but it was never easy to tell with him.

I knew my father was a slow and methodical thinker who needed time to consider things before responding. And what I was telling him would probably take some time to sink in.

As I neared the end of my story and informed my father that I was in Ethiopia, he paused for several seconds before asking, "Can you hitch a ride home?" I smiled to myself; my father had no idea of the vast distances involved here—he had never heard of places like Dubai or even the Middle East. Like my grandfather, he could never bring himself to believe that the world and its phenomena were larger and more complicated than what he understood from his own experience. I knew it was how they thought of the world's potential for evil as well. I remembered what Queen Victoria used to say about such men who frequented the Big Ground brothel: they were perfect marks.

But I also knew that, down deep, my father was a good and decent man. I wondered if that was why I wanted to blame him for everything that had happened to me—because I had always assumed that his basic goodness would protect me. But that was a child's way of thinking, I thought, and I was anything but a child now. Realizing that my father's moral strength was also his vulnerability, I felt an overwhelming rush of both pity and love for him. "I do not blame you for what has happened to me," I blurted out. "And now I know it was wrong for me to do that. I have let that heaviness go from my heart. I know that you are not to blame." And then, because it felt right, I added, "I am free." I was not quite certain if I was referring to my personal freedom or freedom from the guilt in my heart so I could move forward with my life. But it was probably both.

There was a long pause on the other end of the phone. Finally, my father, perhaps recognizing that I had forgiven him without actually speaking the words, replied, "I am sorry, my daughter."

For the first time since arriving in Ethiopia, I felt a strong desire to return home to Namibia. Until that moment, I had been uncertain where I was meant to be; but my father's words were like a beacon pointing the way home.

Almost immediately, we began discussing my return. After I explained to my father that I would have to fly on a plane, he responded with a sudden firmness that Gerson would pay for it. He was the only member of the family who had that kind of money, he said, and even if he did not, he could always sell the new truck he had just bought. I had my doubts, but my father said that he would visit every chief and headman in the area and call Gerson to a meeting around the Holy Fire. "He cannot say anything," my father said flatly. There was a hint of anger in his voice that I had never heard before. "He will only say yes."

And in the end, my father was right. During the meeting with the chiefs and headmen, the decision was made to have Gerson pay for my flight home. He had little choice but to agree to everything; he was peppered with questions about his association with Angel, and his answers aroused so much suspicion that by the time the traditional authorities were finished with him, even he had to admit some degree of guilt. It was generally agreed that there was much more to the story than Gerson was willing to divulge, and many people believed that he lost his honor around the Holy Fire that day.

Finally, it was time for me to visit the Namibian embassy in Addis Ababa; I needed to somehow obtain a passport and whatever paperwork I needed to return home. As I struggled to explain my situation to a low-level clerk at the counter, an embassy official approached and asked me in Otjiherero, "*Peri vi?*" (How are you?) Astonished, I replied, "*Motja vi?*" (What do you want to say?) The man smiled and glanced at the clerk, who was filling in some form with information I had been giving him, and said facetiously, "*Omuzandü nguí má tjangá ombapíra ko"mítiri yé.*" (This boy is writing a letter to his teacher.) He winked and motioned for me to follow him.

He led me to a spacious office, where he had me sit and recount my entire story. When I finished, the man simply stood up, excused himself, and walked out. He returned in about thirty minutes and told me, "You must come back next week. All of your documents will be ready." Noting my astonishment, he told me that he was sorry for what had happened to me, but he knew when he first saw me that I had suffered a great deal. "You are Himba and a daughter of Namibia, so it is my responsibility to help you," he said, adding that he would personally see that everything was taken care of. I thanked him repeatedly and promised to deliver a bag of gifts to his children back in Windhoek. It was the only favor he asked in return. As I was leaving and still trying to express my gratitude, he waved his hand as if it were nothing, smiled warmly, and took me by the arm, saying, *"Ngamwa otjina tji yanda."* (Everything has an end.)

It had been three and half long years since my abduction, but to me the end seemed to come very quickly. Within two months of the initial phone call to my parents, I was boarding a plane home. Saying goodbye to Almaz was difficult; we had been through much together and grown very close. I trusted my friend more than anyone else now. In fact, she was the only person who made me feel like there were still individuals in the world who could be trusted. Almaz even managed to pay me back all the money I had invested in her business, and then some. My friend had found her calling and was full of different ideas for business ventures, still hoping that I would somehow be involved in the future. She promised to visit me in Namibia very soon. On the day of my departure, we embraced one last time. "God bless you, sister," Almaz said.

And with those words, I returned home.

EPILOGUE

It is 2018 and I have been back in Namibia for almost eight years now. I am twenty-seven years old. I live in Windhoek, my country's capital city, where I can live a life of relative anonymity yet still call upon a large network of extended kin when needed. These relationships are important for getting by in a country where a common part of greeting strangers is to work out exactly how you are related. Most of the time, however, I keep to myself. When friends come to see me, it is as if I cannot see them. I am often enveloped in my own solitude.

I had never even been to Windhoek before, and I laugh to myself whenever I think of the route I took to finally get here. As my grandfather used to say, there is a short road and a long road to everywhere. I took the long road to Windhoek. But once here, I have found so much of life—the sights, the sounds, even the smells—familiar. Everything, it seems, has a memory. Sometimes, I wonder what this city would be like if I had never been abducted and instead had come straight here from Opuwo. I think it would have been the most exotic and frightening place I had ever known. But now? Now it is just home. My home.

I work as a seamstress for a distant aunt who runs a dressmaking business. We specialize in making the famous traditional dresses worn by Herero women, a tribe closely related to the Himba. Their Victorian-inspired dresses—called Ohorokova—have a long and cherished history in Namibia. The dresses themselves are highly elaborate, voluminous creations worn over a layered maze of petticoats. They are made with an array of colorful embellishments, including a stunning headdress where the cloth is folded over and over in a particular way to make two long points symbolizing cow horns. In this manner, the women pay homage to the animals that are so central to both Herero and Himba culture. I love to work with all the different kinds of fabrics that come from all over and blanket our tiny shop in a billowing explosion of layered colors and patterns. My favorites are Chitenge from Zambia and Shweshwe from South Africa. When I create Ohorokova out of these rich African textiles, I like to think that I am making some kind of magical shield for women, something that will protect them from everything I experienced.

The chiefs and headmen from my area have watched over me since my return. They inquire after me all the time, even appointing an intermediary—a truck driver whose route takes him between the Kunene and Windhoek—to look in on me now and then. On one such visit, he delivered a plastic bag crammed with Namibian dollars, money raised by the traditional authorities to help me get back on my feet. I could hardly believe it. That money allowed me to begin classes at a local university. I am now two years into getting a business management degree. By continuing my education, I know that I am creating my own personal shield.

I received money from my uncle Gerson as well. I was told that the money came from the sale of his truck, something the chiefs and head-men, on the advice of my father, pressured him to do. But as far as seeing my uncle again, I must go by what my head and my heart are telling me, and both say to stay away. People are not always what they seem. The rumors about his true involvement in my abduction are too strong to ignore. In his pursuit of money and a modern life, he has completely abandoned the old way of doing things. Not everything about the old ways is bad, just like not everything about the new ways is good. It is like my father and my uncle are watching the same herd of cows from opposite sides of a field, and I have spent time with each, seeing the herd through their eyes only. But I know now that the best view is from the center. That is where I will sit.

I did not return to the Kunene until I had already been back in Namibia a year. I associated the region with my childhood and a time when I was ignorant of the evil in this world. And I felt I had moved forward with my life. I also hated how people there gossiped about me now, spreading rumors that almost always had to do with witchcraft, as if I were to blame for what they thought they knew about me. But mostly I think I was just putting off seeing my father.

───────────

When I finally did visit the Kunene, my father insisted that he be the first to see me. We were going to meet in Opuwo, but when I finally arrived I learned that the truck that was supposed to bring my father to town had broken down, so he had decided to walk the remaining one hundred kilometers or so. Nobody knew exactly where he was, and he did not own a phone. But I was not really worried; for a Himba man like my father, walking such distances across the Kunene was nothing, it was normal. Even so, I felt I should at least try to meet him halfway, so I phoned a cousin whose boyfriend had a car, and we set out in his general direction.

We slowly made our way along the lonely back roads of my home area, passing isolated villages and the occasional donkey cart. The dirt roads were heavily corrugated and in some places completely washed out by recent flooding. It had been raining in the Kunene, and a thin glaze of faded green grass sprouted up between the red rocks to cloak the lacerated countryside. To most outsiders, it must have looked like nothing, but to me it seemed like the Kunene had been transformed.

We were crossing a wide, flat stretch of desert plain when I spotted a lonely figure walking on the side of the road directly ahead of us. At first, he was just a wavy apparition in the rippling heat of the afternoon, but eventually I made out the sparse attire of a Himba man: walking stick, sandals, cloth skirt—and on his upper body a tattered sport jacket with no shirt. As we drew closer, I recognized the determined, steady gait of my father.

After going through the customary greetings, my cousin and her boyfriend decided to drive to a nearby village to find something to drink, informing us that they would return in a couple of hours. So my father and I walked off to sit in the shade of a group of mopani trees. We talked for a long time, mostly about family: how excited my mother was to see me, how my brothers were doing, the latest news about different aunts, uncles, and cousins. I had already heard about my grandfather, who had died just six months after my abduction. According to my father, the Old One would not stop talking about me toward the end. He spoke constantly of being able to hear my vibrations through the ground; vibrations that grew increasingly faint, which made him think that something had gone terribly wrong. It was my grandfather who finally convinced my father that leaving me in Angola was a mistake and that he should return to look for me before it was too late.

When my father came home without me, my grandfather was as devastated as anyone. He refused to eat and fell into a long depression. Ultimately, he became ill, though nobody could say exactly what was wrong with him. Even the local healer, who never failed to identify the cause of a person's misfortune, was for once perplexed by my grandfather's condition. But one night, as my father sat alone by my grandfather's side, the Old One confided in him that he was not really sick at all; he had simply made a decision to move on. "I must go and call upon the elephants to find my granddaughter," he whispered to my father. "It is the only way to help her and bring her home." To this day, I am certain that it was my grandfather, at the head of a thousand charging elephants, who ultimately rescued me.

My father grew silent as he stared out across the broad, windswept valley surrounding us. He sifted sand absentmindedly through his heavily callused fingers. Finally, he said distantly, as if to himself, "A man does not start his farming with cattle, he starts it with people." I knew the phrase—it was an old Himba proverb. I had heard it many times before. Shifting his gaze downward, my father stared intently at the finely granulated sand in his hand, as if reading a book. There was another long silence. "I have failed you, my daughter," my father said, looking up at me. "I have failed my family. And I will live with that failure every time the sun rises. Each time I see your face, I will know that the suffering I see there is due to me." He turned away and looked in the opposite direction. I knew that he was crying, but I remained silent. It would have been embarrassing for him if I tried to console him. Besides, I was trying to compose myself.

After a few minutes, when I thought we had both recovered, I said, "As I told you on the phone, my father, I have truly let go of these things. Now that we are here together, I know this is true. The darkness in my heart is gone—at least when it comes to holding that darkness against other people—against you." I told my father about the healer in Addis Ababa and how I was now moving forward with my life. I told him what I knew to be true; I told him what was important for him to know. But I did not tell him everything.

My father said he would return to the village. I offered to drive him back, but he wanted to walk. So we said our goodbyes, and I began making my way back to the road. I glanced back once, and the image of that moment—of my father sitting under the mopani tree—will stay with me forever. It is the image I associate with everything that I did not tell him. What did I hold back? It is this: that though it was true that I forgave him, it was also true that our relationship was forever changed. While you can forgive someone something, it does not mean that its presence is gone; it is still there, and the relationship is changed because of it. But I believe my father understood that too.

After the meeting with my father, the path was clear for me to connect with the rest of my family. We held a big event with over a hundred people in attendance. The number of friends and extended family members who made the trip to Opuwo to see me was truly overwhelming. There were as many as six cooking fires with over twenty large cast-iron potjie pots all filled with different stews and meats. The aroma alone brought back all the good memories of my childhood.

So many things had changed over the course of a few years. I met relatives I had not seen since I was a little girl, and some I did not even know I had. While I was away, my brother Timo had gotten married. He now had a two-year-old boy and a newborn baby girl. My other brothers were so grown up that I hardly recognized them. As for my mother, she remained by my side the entire time. Each time she looked into my eyes, she began to cry. And she never let go of my hand, as if afraid that I might float away if she did. Throughout the party, the older people kept filling my pockets with handfuls of soil—the red ocher sand of Himbaland—to ensure that the ancestors remained close and always watched over me.

As is the tendency among the Himba during such get-togethers, the men and women eventually drifted apart and separated into two groups. I sat with the women under a huge marula tree. I expected the usual topics of conversation: small talk, family gossip, or news from everyone's home villages and wherever they had just traveled from. But something unanticipated and truly wonderful happened. The conversation turned lively and became unlike anything I had ever heard before. It was new and surprising. It began among the younger women, but the older ones, after listening and nodding their heads in agreement for a while, became actively engaged too. Soon, everyone was contributing and clamoring to speak, wanting to get their words out, as if they could no longer hold back whatever it was that had been growing inside of them for a very long time.

And what was this conversation about? It was about who we are as Himba women and what our place is in a rapidly changing world, a world that holds both immense promise and infinite risks. Though the remote desert expanses of the Kunene might make it seem like it, we are no longer isolated. We touch the world and the world touches us. As women, we cannot allow ourselves to be victims in this process; we cannot just sit by our cooking fires and expect our men to always protect us and look out for our best interests. Traditionally, we have always understood that we are capable of voicing our own interests in our villages and communities when we unite as a group. But now our world is so much more than the village and the community. And the issues involved are more than motherhood and domestic life and everything else that we as women have traditionally been concerned about.

But as we talked about these things it felt like our words were somehow wrong. They were disjointed, scattered, as if they did not truly belong to the group. People began to quarrel and talk over one another.

And then my great-auntie spoke. She was a quiet, old woman whose true age nobody really knew. But she was my grandfather's eldest sister and everyone respected her. When she spoke, it was like entering a library.

"Daughter," she said, turning to me, "go stand there in the middle." We were sitting in a large circle under the canopy of the marula tree, so I got up and placed myself at the center. "Do you see how she stands there among us?" my auntie said, pointing her walking stick at me from her seated position at the base of the tree. "She stands at the center of our family. And because she is a woman, we who are both family and women have the strongest bond with her. We are the first and most important circle. And around this circle is a larger circle that is the village. And around that circle is a larger one still that is the Himba tribe. It was not until recently that we even knew about circles that go beyond this, circles that include Namibia, Africa, and the world. But even then, we have been content to let the men deal with them; as women we have not acted beyond the circles of family, village, and tribe. But now I think what we are saying is that this can no longer be the case. If we are to survive as Himba, as Namibians, as Africans, as people of this world, then the women must participate like never before. We must unite and let our voices be heard. I am too old to know the best way to do this. It is for the younger generations. But I can say one thing: whatever we do, we must do it from the innermost circle out. Then we do it our way, from our strengths, and in a way that preserves our traditions. Otherwise, bad things happen, like what happened to our daughter here. The closest circles around her—those of family and village and tribe—they were smashed and broken because our women have not participated in those larger circles. We have been silent. This must change, but it must do so from here, from the innermost circle out."

Later that evening, I climbed one of the flat-topped etendekas surrounding Opuwo. I wound my way past gigantic termite mounds and passed through scattered forests of black thorn and mopani, the distinctive butterfly-shaped leaves of the latter cracking under my feet. I scrambled up and over clusters of craggy volcanic rock that must have been millions of years old. When I reached the top, the sun was just about to set. From my vantage point, I could look out across the mountain ranges of the Central Plateau and the Great Escarpment toward the horizon, where the Northern Namib Desert meets the cold waters of the Atlantic Ocean. I thought about my great-auntie's words and how they were like little points of light connecting who I once was to everything I wanted to become. They reconciled me with my past and brought hope to my life. So as I watched the sun set that evening, I knew it would rise again tomorrow.

———————

Now, when I think back on what happened to me, I cannot always make sense of it. I think the potential for evil in this world is very powerful and that it feeds forces we find difficult to understand. There are vast yet mostly unknown networks of well-organized and overlapping groups that profit from the slave trade, or what most people now call human trafficking. In Namibia, we know the term *trafficking* from its association with rhino horns. But when it comes to humans, we seem to be silent. I think it is because we do not believe—or do not want to believe—that such evil can visit our homes and cooking fires. Even when I myself try to comprehend the true power of the people involved in human trafficking, it leaves me stunned. It is frightening to think how expansive and well coordinated their operations have to be for a man in Dubai to be able to satisfy his sexual appetites with relative ease by literally ordering a Himba girl from southwestern Africa.

I often come back to the letter Rakesh wrote me prior to his suicide, in which he, too, highlighted far-reaching yet largely unknown forces working against him. I agree with what he said about how difficult it is to fight such forces. But it is not impossible. I am a living example of how one person can fight back, survive, and eventually move forward with her life. So now I live to bear witness. I want my story to serve as another kind of shield to protect people and show them how to live with a noble heart.

Until now, I have not told many people what happened to me. Some say that I have been silent because I am filled with shame and fear. They say that I should continue to hide my story. They say that I should just wait for my death. But I do not believe any of this. Since I have moved forward with my life, I do not experience shame or fear. I have more to do than simply wait for my death. I am not a poor, suffering girl from Africa. I am a Himba woman from Namibia. I am an elephant walker. I am a shield maker.